party of five™

A Family Album

party of five™

A Family Album

Wendy Corsi Staub

BERKLEY BOULEVARD BOOKS, NEW YORK

PARTY OF FIVE: A FAMILY ALBUM

A Berkley Boulevard Book/ published by arrangement with
Sony Signatures, Inc.

Based on the television series created by Christopher Keyser & Amy Lippman

PRINTING HISTORY
Berkley Boulevard trade paperback edition / March 1998

The Penguin Putnam Inc. World Wide Web site address is
http://www.penguinputnam.com

ISBN: 0-425-16495-0

BERKLEY BOULEVARD
Berkley Boulevard Books are published by The Berkley Publishing Group,
a member of Penguin Putnam Inc.,
200 Madison Avenue, New York, New York 10016.
BERKLEY BOULEVARD and its logo are trademarks
belonging to Berkley Publishing Corporation.

PRINTED IN THE UNITED STATES OF AMERICA

10   9   8   7   6   5   4   3   2   1

Bailey,

I was going through some boxes in the attic the other day, looking for this picture of Mom and Dad — the one that was taken at the surprise party we threw for their twenty-fifth anniversary. You know, the one someone snapped right when they walked into the restaurant and saw us all there. Mom's all teary and happy and Dad's mouth is wide open in shock.

I don't know exactly why I needed that particular picture. I guess I was just thinking about it, and I got to wondering where it was, and I felt like looking at it. But I couldn't find it. At least, not right away. I must've gone through, like, fifty or sixty boxes and trunks until I finally found it in with a bunch of pregnancy pamphlets from when Mom was expecting Owen.

Anyway, I realized that it might be a good idea to start keeping track of stuff like that — pictures, and letters, and mementos — so that every thing is organized in one place. So that, whenever one of us is feeling nostalgic, we can, without having to rip closets and dresser drawers apart, sit down and look back at the way things are. I mean, were.

We're going to do that, you know. Look back, I mean. Because the older we get, the more things are going to change. We won't always be living together, all five of us, in this house, the way we are now. But that doesn't mean we should forget what it was like – or how important it is to hang on to each other, no matter what. Because, when you come right down to it, all we've ever had, since Mom and Dad died, is each other. And it seems important to create some sort of record, something that will be around after these days are gone.

Granted, these haven't always been the best of times. But that doesn't mean we should forget the problems or the pain. Instead, we should try to remember it. All of it. That's what Mom and Dad did for us – and would have kept on doing. They shared pieces of their lives, and used their pasts to help shape our futures.

So that's why I think we should put together a family scrapbook. We can fill it with anything that seems meaningful, anything that helps to document these past few years. Because someday all this will mean so much.

Love,

-Julia

DRUNK DRIVING ACCIDENT CLAIMS TWO VICTIMS

BY GREG HYLAND
STAFF REPORTER

A San Francisco couple lost their lives in a two-car accident on Saturday night. Nick Salinger, 47, and his wife, Diana Gordon Salinger, 45, were killed instantly when their vehicle was struck broadside at the intersection of California Street and Van Ness Avenue at 8:22 p.m. The second car, operated by Walter Alcott, 42, of Powell Street, failed to stop at a red light. Alcott, who wasn't injured in the accident, was charged with driving while intoxicated and taken into custody at the scene.

Salinger was co-owner of the popular restaurant on Union Street that bears his name. According to Joe Mangus, his business partner, the victims were on their way to a concert at Symphony Hall when the accident occurred. "This is a terrible, terrible tragedy," the distraught Mangus stated. "They were wonderful people. I am just devastated...by this loss."

Diana Salinger was a concert violinist of national renown. The couple, who celebrated their twenty-sixth wedding anniversary in January, are survived by five children: Charles, 23; Bailey, 15; Julia, 14; Claudia, 11; and Owen, 8 months. Emmet Graham, the family's attorney, would not comment on who will be named the guardian for the four younger children, all of whom are living at home.

Alcott, owner of a North Beach bookstore, will be arraigned today.

WALTER
What can I do? Tell me what can I do?

JULIA
There's nothing. But I know what you want from me. You want me to forgive you.

WALTER
Yes.

JULIA
I don't know if I *can* do that. I mean, it wasn't just my life you changed. I don't know if I have the right to speak for anyone else... And what does that even mean, to say I forgive you? Will it change anything? Or does it just mean not being angry at you anymore—not hating you? Because I want that so much, just as much as you. I'll try. I'm gonna try. The only thing I can do...is tell you we're gonna be okay. Because we are, the five of us. I don't know how I know that, but I do. We're gonna be okay. And maybe if you know that, you'll be okay, too.

BAILEY
Look, when can you start?
NANNY CANDIDATE
I have...a few questions first. I think it's essential that my child-rearing philosophy coincides with the family's. For example, I'm from the developmental school. I believe in allowing a child to progress at his own pace—with emphasis on building self-esteem.
BAILEY
That would be great! Self-esteem would be great!
NANNY CANDIDATE
What about potty training? Do you plan to force the issue, or permit Owen to say when he's ready?
BAILEY
Actually, my sister Claudia cleans up most of the poop around here. You ought to ask her that question.
NANNY CANDIDATE
Have you read any Piaget?
BAILEY
Piaget? I don't think... Tell me how it starts, and maybe I'll remember.

WANTED: Nanny for adorable one-year-old orphan. Must be available five days per week, some evenings. Lite housework, laundry, cooking. Live out. References required. Call 555-7824 after three p.m.

BABYSITTER, reliable energetic 2 active boys, have car. St. ~~~

October 10

I won this scholarship award at school today— the Knights of Pythagoras award. It's kind of a big deal— only one person wins it every year, and it's this engraved trophy and a check to put toward college expenses. But all I could think of, when Principal Stickley was handing it over to me and making a big speech about all my academic and extracurricular achievements, and the newspaper photographer was snapping a picture for the paper, was that Mom and Dad weren't there to see it, and how meaningless it felt without them. I mean, they should have been there. It's so unfair that they weren't. They lived for this kind of stuff. They were always in the front row, cheering, at Bailey's football games, and whenever Claudia performed... That's the kind of parents they were. And now, it's like, anything good that happens to any of us isn't worth nearly as much as it once would have. And I can't help wondering if it's always gonna be this way. Because if it is... why bother? Why bother trying to do anything good, or achieve anything special? Because they'd want me to, that's what I keep trying to tell myself. But somehow, that answer just doesn't seem good enough anymore. And I don't know where to turn for one that is.

BAILEY
I'm feeling my way through this—same as you.

JULIA
Do you think about them, Bailey?

BAILEY
Course I do.

JULIA
Well, why don't you talk about it? Why don't we ever talk about them?

BAILEY
Maybe because we think we gotta be brave for Claud and Owen. But maybe that's stupid. Maybe we should talk about it. Maybe it would help.

JULIA
Sometimes I wonder if this feeling's ever gonna go away.

BAILEY
I don't know. I hope so. But I don't know.

CLAUDIA

You only look at what we do wrong.

MRS. GIDEON

I don't think so, sweetheart.

CLAUDIA

What about all the stuff we do right? Like the fact that Bailey gets up in the middle of the night—a couple of times every night—for Owen? I mean, he's sixteen, and on Friday nights, he baby-sits.

MRS. GIDEON

Claudia—

CLAUDIA

Julia trims my bangs. And she doesn't let me watch movies on cable. And Charlie has this rule about vegetables with dinner. And Bailey came on this field trip with my class, to the Planetarium, with like three other mothers. And they make me get my teeth cleaned twice a year. And we all take turns reading to Owen. And I'm trying to think of everything else—

MRS. GIDEON

Claudia—

CLAUDIA

I don't know what you want from us. Tell me—what more are we supposed to do? Are we supposed to be perfect?

MRS. GIDEON

Of course not.

CLAUDIA

Are there many families who do that much better?... We made it through the last nine months. I don't think it can get much harder than that. Do you? The only thing that's going to ruin this for us, and that's gonna stop us from being a family, is you.

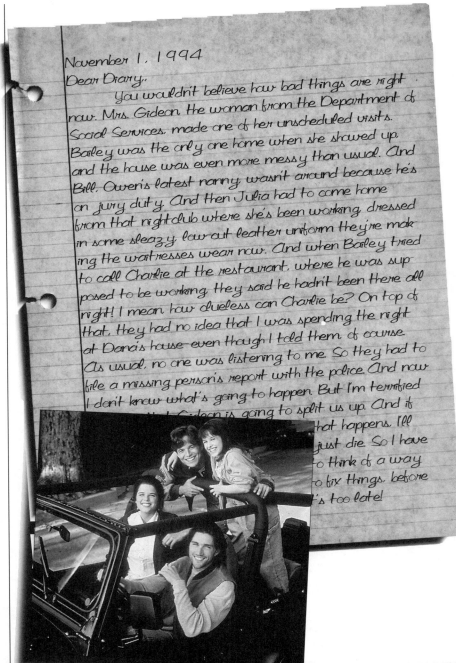

November 1, 1994

Dear Diary,

You wouldn't believe how bad things are right now. Mrs. Gideon, the woman from the Department of Social Services, made one of her unscheduled visits. Bailey was the only one home when she showed up, and the house was even more messy than usual. And Bill, Owen's latest nanny, wasn't around because he's on jury duty. And then Julia had to come home from that nightclub where she's been working, dressed in some sleazy, low-cut leather uniform they're making the waitresses wear now. And when Bailey tried to call Charlie at the restaurant, where he was supposed to be working, they said he hadn't been there all night! I mean how clueless can Charlie be? On top of that, they had no idea that I was spending the night at Dana's house—even though I told them, of course. As usual, no one was listening to me. So they had to file a missing person's report with the police. And now I don't know what's going to happen. But I'm terrified [Mrs.] Gideon is going to split us up. And if [t]hat happens, I'll [?] just die. So I have [?] to think of a way [?] to fix things, before [?][i]t's too late!

BAILEY
I don't want to *make* you do this.

KATE
You're not. I told you. I want us to.

BAILEY
Why? Why are you doing this?

KATE
Because. I'm going away. And you won't be driving me to school every morning, and you won't be calling me every night before you go to bed anymore. We won't have any of that stuff—you know, that stuff that seems like it doesn't mean anything, but it really means—kind of everything. And I don't know, you know, we'll write to each other but still...you'll meet other people. Other girls. And maybe you'll start to forget about me. But if we have this—you know, instead of all that other stuff—maybe you won't forget. Maybe it'll keep us together.

BAILEY
No. No. I'm...sorry. I don't know what's gonna happen with us, Kate, but you're gonna be away for a really long time, and—well, I have this image of Hotchkiss being full of really good-looking, athletic, smart guys. And they're gonna all want to go out with you. And for you to give up something so important, just to try to hang on to me—well, that just doesn't make sense. Cause someday you'll decide to spend the rest of your life with a guy. And you know you want to look at him and tell him he's the only one.

KATE
Maybe that guy'll be you.

BAILEY
Yeah. Maybe.

Dear Kate:

By now you should be settled in at Hotchkiss, since you left over a week ago. Is it weird, sleeping over at school? I never knew anyone who went to boarding school, and it just seems like it might be. Weird, I mean.

I miss you so bad, Kate. I keep thinking about what happened the night before you left. I keep wondering what it would be like if I hadn't said no. If we had done it, maybe you would have called me or written by now. Then again, maybe it would make you feel obligated to call or write, when in the end it's going to be better if we just let it fade away. Is that what you want? I hate this— not seeing you, not talking to you, not knowing how you feel.

Please, Kate, get in touch and let me know if it's over, or if it just feels like it is and I'm making too much out of things. I know it'll never be like it used to be between us, with you so far away. But I still want you in my life, if you want to be there.

Love,

Bailey

October 24, 1982.
Nick and the boys
took Avery and me
to the airport.
Julia cried when I
kissed her good-bye.
An awkward moment between Nick
and Avery at the gate. The flight was coast-
to-coast turbulence. Avery held my hand the
whole way and made me listen to a very bad recording of Mendelssohn on the airplane headphones. It
helped.

October 22:
Avery insisted we knock off rehearsal early and go
for a walk. We ended up on the Upper West
Side in a used bookstore. He bought me this
ancient edition of Dantes Inferno. I read the
Paolo and Francesca chapter when I got back to my
room. So romantic. I just called home but Nicks
putting the kids to bed and can't talk.

November 1:
The recording session is over. Seven takes of the
Handel — my fault all of them, but Avery
got me through it. At the postmortem party, I
watched him across the room, and when he smiled
at me, this beautiful, warm smile, I actually looked
over my shoulder because I assumed it was meant
for someone else. We slipped out a back exit and
took a carriage ride around the park. Around and
around ...

JULIA
So my mother had an affair.
With you. I mean, I should know
that. So I don't walk around
thinking my parents had this
perfect marriage.

AVERY
We didn't have an affair,
Julia.

JULIA
You said you were in love with
her. You *told* me.

AVERY
I was in love with her.

JULIA
And she was in love with you! I
read her journals. I know. I
know about New York.

AVERY
New York... Maybe she was in
love with me. I'd like to
believe that. But you want to
know the truth? The truth was
it was a beautiful night, and
we'd just played Bach better
then we'd ever played it in our
lives, and we had too much to
drink and had too many people
tell us we were wonderful and
she was in this long black
dress, and she'd lost her bar-
rette somewhere on Sixth Avenue
and her hair was whipping all
over the place and she was
thirty-two and away from home
and I told her I was in love
with her—and for a second it
might have happened... But we
got back to the hotel—and the
room was filled with flowers.
Dozens of flowers. From your
father. And there was a note.
She wouldn't show it to me. But
it made her laugh. She just sat
there on the bed and laughed
and laughed. And I knew I'd
lost her.

ROSS

You're a better violinist than I am.

CLAUDIA

Oh, please. I am not. Duh! You're a great violinist. Tell you what, I'll play it again. This time, *pay attention*.

ROSS

I don't need to hear it again. And even if I did, I can't think of anything I could possibly tell you that would help you make the leap from great to brilliant... I think you need a new teacher. We both knew this was gonna happen sooner or later.

CLAUDIA

But *you're* my teacher.

ROSS

I've taught you everything I know, Claud. I think you need to move on to someone who can take your playing to the next level. Because I *can't*. That's why I played one of your practice tapes for Gloria Metzler.

CLAUDIA

Gloria...Metzler?

ROSS

You remember. We saw her in concert last year at Davies Hall? She only takes two or three students a year and...well, she's agreed to take you. This is a good thing, Claud. You're on your way.

ELEVEN-YEAR-OLD PERFORMS WITH ENSEMBLE

Fifth-grader Claudia Salinger wins raves for her first professional performance.

RICHARD SILLETT
STAFF REPORTER

Claudia Salinger may be in the fifth grade, but she already achieved something many grown musicians only dream about. Last weekend, the budding violinist became the youngest performer ever to take the stage with the Bay Area Chamber Ensemble.

Claudia had been playing the violin for six years. According to her instructor, Ross Anderson, "Claudia is one of the most gifted violinists I have ever seen. She has incredible talent, along with dedication and discipline that are remarkable not only for someone her age, but for anyone who has been through what she has this year."

He is, of course, referring to the fact that Claudia's parents, Nick and Diana Salinger, were tragically killed by a drunk driver in an automobile accident last March. Claudia, along with her infant brother, Owen, and teenage brother and sister, Bailey and Julia, are now being raised by her oldest brother, Charles, 24.

"She definitely takes after her mother," Claudia's guardian says with a smile, when asked about his sister's exceptional musical aptitude. Indeed, the late Diana Salinger, who performed under her maiden name, Diana Gordon, was a nationally renowned violinist who often performed with the Bay Area Chamber Ensemble. Her bittersweet legacy was evident at Symphony Hall this past weekend, as her youngest daughter's flawless performance brought tears to the eyes of family and close friends who were in the audience.

Bailey Salinger, who watched his sister from the front row with little Owen in his lap, commented, "You can listen to Claudia, and you know that our mother is still with us."

When asked about her amazing talent, the pint-sized musician merely shrugs. "I just love to play, that's all," she says with a smile. "It makes me happy."

Dear Jill,

I just wanted to apologize again for las[t] night.. I can't believe my brother th[inks] he can show up in my room whenever [he] feels like it. Even though we got caught, I wanted you to know tha[t] what happened with us was really s[pe]cial to me. In case you couldn't te[ll], I've never done it before. Or m[aybe] you could tell— I have no idea.

Anyway, I thought I should tell you. And now [that] the first time is behind me, I'm not so nervous anymore. In fact, I'm not nervous at all. I can't wait to be alone with you again. I was thinking— maybe tonight? Maybe at your house? Because we definitely can't count on Charlie for any privacy. I can't believe what he's turning into. He used to be a pretty cool guy, but lately he's all uptight. And like I said last night, I swear it isn't you. How can anyone not like you? Charlie just acts like he doesn't want you around because he's on this power trip lately, I guess. Don't let it bother you. Because no matter what, I want you around. All the time.

See you after school.

Love,

Bailey

BAILEY
You can't just bust in my room—

CHARLIE
Claudia's downstairs, for God's sake!

BAILEY
Claudia's downstairs when you and Kirsten are doing it.

CHARLIE
That's not the same thing.

BAILEY
It's exactly the same.

CHARLIE
Claudia's downstairs, you're sixteen, you can't have sex in this house.

BAILEY
You had sex in this house when you were sixteen.

CHARLIE
Not much, I didn't. Mom and Dad made it impossible for me and I'm going to make it impossible for you.

BAILEY
Oh, like that's fair.

JILL
Don't you get it? I can't trust you.

BAILEY
You can't trust *me*? What is that, a joke?

JILL
Yeah. It's a riot. I can't tell you how much I'm enjoying this. What lovely surprise have you arranged for me next, Bailey? When are the guys in the white coats coming to take me away?

BAILEY
Jill. You need help.

JILL
We used to have fun, remember? And now this is the only thing we're about. Well, I don't need this. Why don't you just go to hell, huh?

Bailey:
That was a lousy thing you did telling my mother. I have a problem for your information: I am not "on drugs." I've tried a few things a couple of times but who hasn't? You? I guess I never knew you were such a straight arrow. Whatever. From now on, you do your thing, Bailey and I'll do mine. But it's not going to be around here. Thanks to you my mother's making my life miserable: smelling my breath, checking my pupils— what a drag. I always wanted to check out the scene in L.A. anyway. Now's the time. So I'll see you around… or maybe I won't. I guess you'll figure it's no great loss though huh? You wouldn't want a druggie like me hanging around would you? God, I can't believe this is happening to us. I really thought we had something great Bay. Too bad you blew it.

Jill

Julia

Drew and I were wondering if you were up to having a few people over to your place again tonight. His mom's apartment is too small and his kid sisters always hanging around and my parents are still pissed at me for the last time I had people over (someone kinda broke the frame on their bed). Anyway since you're the only one we know with your own place—sort of—we figured you were the logical person to ask. Let us know before last period so we can spread the word. Oh, and maybe this time we won't have to invite your friend Lilly. Don't get me wrong, it's not that I don't like her—but she kind of puts a damper on things. See you in Geometry!

Nina

DR. WEEKS

Straight A's for three straight years. Then suddenly, we start seeing some B's, couple C's...

JULIA

Those are passing grades.

DR. WEEKS

And unexcused absences.

JULIA

A lot of kids cut classes.

DR. WEEKS

You're not a lot of kids, Julia. Look, I want to talk about how the last few months have been for you.

JULIA

They've been great. Thanks.

DR. WEEKS

Listen. When you and I talked right after your parents' accident, we talked about some of the things you could expect to feel—I'm looking at your record here, and I'm seeing someone who is really angry, and pulling away hard from all the things that used to matter to her. So listen, what I'd like to do, if you're okay with it, is to set up a time for you and me to talk about those feelings. Maybe if we explore it a little, we can help you find some enthusiasm for those things that used to really mean a lot to you. How does that sound?

JULIA

You said this was optional, right?

December 12, 1994

Dear Diary,

Now that Artie and I have been going out for some time, I've realized it's time to think about the future. Namely, the possibility that we'll get married someday, after we've both gotten through junior high and high school and college. According to Artie, the statistics on the failure rate of mixed marriages are staggering. We may be only eleven but it's always a good idea to plan ahead. So I've made an important decision. I've decided to convert to Judaism. After all, I don't feel all that attached to being an Episcopalian, and Mom and Dad were never big on going to church. And Charlie never makes us go. I just hope nobody freaks out when I tell them...

CLAUDIA
Blessed art thou, oh, Lord, our God, who commands us to kindle—

JULIA
—Claudia? *What* are you doing?

CLAUDIA
The prayer over the Sabbath candles.

JULIA
Excuse me?

CLAUDIA
I wanted to do it in Hebrew, and they've got this funny translation, but I can't quite get it right. See—"Barook ata adoonay, eloohaynu—"

JULIA
—Claudia? *Why* are you doing this?

CLAUDIA
You mean because it isn't Sabbath?

JULIA
I mean because you aren't Jewish.

CLAUDIA

Oh. You're still alive.

BAILEY

Of course we are. What are you talking about?

CLAUDIA

In case you missed it, we had an aftershock almost three hours ago.

JULIA

What...? God, Claud. It was tiny.

BAILEY

Yeah, you could barely feel it.

CLAUDIA

I felt it. And the plan was, the ground shakes, call home. Period. I've been sitting by the phone and watching the news to make sure you weren't trapped in some collapsed parking garage! I even tried to call France on the off chance you got confused about the plan. And did anybody bother to call? No!

OFFICIAL SALINGER FAMILY EARTHQUAKE GUIDE
by Claudia Salinger

As we all know, San Francisco is prone to earthquakes. According to the National Seismology Institute, the first 72 hours after the quake are crucial. During this period, there will most likely be aftershocks, or another quake. Therefore, I have come up with the following plan to be put into effect immediately:

Stage 1: Preparation
A. Secure all glassware with Quake-Grip to prevent breakage
B. Strap heavy furniture to walls
C. Ensure that house is bolted securely to its foundation

Stage 2: Ground Shakes
A. Grab Owen
B. If indoors, get into a doorway or under a table
C. If outdoors, move to open space
D. Don't panic!

Stage 3: After It's Over
A. If you are at home, check for damage and man the telephone
B. If you are not at home, call home to report that you're okay
C. If you are not at home and cannot get through on a local line, call Uncle Kurt in France (I okayed this with him and he has agreed to accept collect calls)
D. If you are at home and everyone has not been accounted for within a half-hour, call Uncle Kurt in France to see if he has been contacted
E. If you are not at home, get home as soon as possible (even if the roads are gone)

Charlie Salinger's Broiled Steak with Sauteed Mushrooms and Onions

Ingredients

1 T-Bone steak, about 1 1/2 inches thick
1 clove garlic, cut in half
2 tablespoons butter
1 small onion, thinly sliced
1/2 lb. fresh mushrooms, sliced
Salt
Freshly ground black pepper

Preheat broiler.
Melt butter in frying pan over medium heat.
Prepare steak by rubbing both sides with cut edges of garlic. Discard clove. Place steak three inches from heat source. Broil about 7 minutes for rare, 8 minutes for medium, per side.
While steak is broiling, sauté onions for several minutes until they start to become transparent. Add mushrooms and continue to sauté about five minutes. Remove steak from broiler.
Season generously with salt and pepper. Garnish with onion-mushroom mixture. Serves one.

JULIA

I feel really bad. And I'm trying—

LIBBY

You could've had Justin before, but then he wasn't good enough for you. *Now* he is. Now that he's my boyfriend. *Was.*

JULIA

That's not what happened. Libby, I just...
I couldn't help it.

LIBBY

That is such a lame excuse. If something happened between you and Justin and you were really my friend, you could have said no.

JULIA

That's true. I'm sorry.

LIBBY

Look, Julia. The last thing I need right now is to think about you and Justin feeling sorry for me. Cause frankly that makes me want to throw up.

JULIA

There's nothing I can say?

LIBBY

You don't actually think I'm gonna forgive you, do you? You did what you did. Suffer the consequences. I am. Anyway, I'm sure you and Justin'll find a way to make each other feel better. Know what, Jul—I really hate you for this.

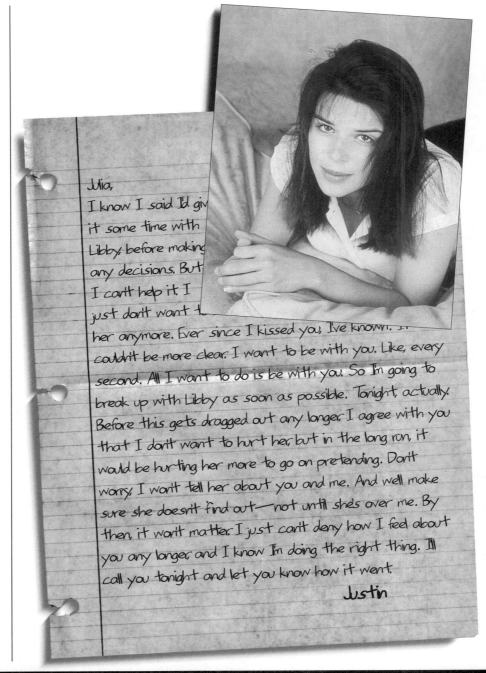

Julia,
I know I said I'd giv[e]
it some time with
Libby, before making
any decisions. But
I can't help it. I
just don't want t[o see]
her anymore. Ever since I kissed you, I've known. It
couldn't be more clear. I want to be with you. Like, every
second. All I want to do is be with you. So I'm going to
break up with Libby as soon as possible. Tonight, actually.
Before this gets dragged out any longer. I agree with you
that I don't want to hurt her, but in the long run, it
would be hurting her more to go on pretending. Don't
worry, I won't tell her about you and me. And we'll make
sure she doesn't find out—not until she's over me. By
then, it won't matter. I just can't deny how I feel about
you any longer, and I know I'm doing the right thing. I'll
call you tonight and let you know how it went.

Justin

CHARLIE
You didn't get her anything either?!

JULIA
I've been busy too!

CHARLIE
Okay. Look—I'll sign a check—you go downtown after school and buy her something.

JULIA
Like what?

CHARLIE
I don't know, something expensive. We'll give it to her tonight.

JULIA
We always do presents at breakfast. She'll be expecting it this morning.

CHARLIE
So we'll just avoid her till you get back.

JULIA
Avoid her? On her *birthday*?

CHARLIE
You got a better idea?

MEMO TO: Charlie, Bailey, Julia and Kirst—
FROM: Claudia
RE: My Birthday

This is just a reminder for those of you who may have lost track of time, since February is a short and exceptionally busy month I will be turning twelve on the day after tomorrow. I have left the evening open, in case anyone assumed I might already have plans. I'll probably just stay at home leafing through catalogues, checking out snowboards, since I thought I might take up the sport. If I had a snowboard. But, since I don't have one and I can't afford to buy one, I guess I won't be doing that any time soon. Also, I'll probably be wearing jeans and a sweater, since there's probably no reason to get dressed up that night. I mean, it's not as though anyone's throwing me a party or anything right??? Anyway, I've outgrown all my dress-up clothes and the stuff Julia handed down to me is out-dated. I sure wish I still had that Nordstrom's gift certificate Bailey gave me for Christmas, but I already used it. That sure was a great gift idea thanks again Bay. Anyway, I hope everyone feels free to stop by my tent for a chat if they have any questions about anything.

P.S. Just thought I'd mention that a list of my thirty seven closest friends, along with their home phone numbers, can be found taped to the outside flap of my tent. In case anyone was wondering.

TEEN DIES OF OVERDOSE

BY JEFF WASSON

STAFF REPORTER

Jill Holbrook, 16, of San Francisco, died of an apparent drug overdose yesterday afternoon at her family's Powell Street apartment.

The deceased, a member of the junior class at Grant High School, was found unconscious in her bedroom by her mother, a registered nurse. An emergency rescue squad responded promptly to a 9-1-1 call placed at 4:31 p.m. by the deceased's older brother, Griffin Holbrook. Attempts to resuscitate her failed, and she was pronounced dead at the scene. An unspecified quantity of cocaine was found in the deceased's possession. An autopsy report will be released at a later date.

BAILEY
I'm not gonna feel that way about anyone anymore. I'm not gonna love anyone anymore.

CHARLIE
Bailey—

BAILEY
—I can't. I can't. I don't want to. *Please.* It's too hard. And it hurts too much. So I don't want to love anyone. And I don't want anyone to love me.

CHARLIE
That's too bad. You don't have a choice—

BAILEY
No—

CHARLIE
Cause I love you, Bay. I love you.

CHARLIE

You're asking me to marry you?

KIRSTEN

Yes! I know you may think this is crazy. And I know I've said no to *you* once—but *forget* about that. I love you. So—*obviously* I want to make a commitment to you forever. Because—what are we waiting for? Huh? I mean, when you have—*now*—exactly what you want—why wait? Things only go away—so I wanna hold on to everything that matters to me...and that means you, Charlie.

CHARLIE

...I wanted to ask you.

KIRSTEN

What?

CHARLIE

I'm supposed to ask you. Damn! Damn! I was getting all ready...

KIRSTEN

Oh, for God's sake! Does that mean yes? Is that what you're saying? Yes?

CHARLIE

Yes. Okay?... Yes... Yes... Yes... I will definitely marry you.

ANNOUNCEMENTS

BETROTHED—A November wedding is being planned for Kirsten Bennett and Charles Salinger, both of San Francisco.

Miss Bennett, the daughter of Mr. and Mrs. Eugene Bennett of Chicago, Illinois, is an alumnus of The Henderson School in Chicago and San Francisco State University. She is currently working on her Ph.D. in Child Psychology and has been employed as a nanny.

Mr. Salinger, the son of the late Nick and Diane Salinger, is a graduate of Grant High School in San Francisco, and attended the University of California at Berkeley. He is employed as the manager of Salinger's Restaurant on Union Street and resides in San Francisco.

STUDENTS DEFY NEW ANTI-KISSING RULE

BY BARRY NEVILLE

Principal Stickley dropped a bomb on Grant High School students during her welcome back speech at last week's assembly. In addition to a new rule that forbids students to eat in the stairwells, she announced that public displays of affection will no longer be allowed on campus. Translation: smooching your significant other in the hallway could get you into big trouble.

That is exactly what happened to two unfortunate members of the Junior Class. When Ms. Stickley caught Julia Salinger and Justin Thompson kissing each other by Julia's locker after school on Tuesday afternoon, she gave them detention.

Undaunted, the couple launched a campaign to fight the new rule, issuing petitions and passing out flyers announcing "The Big Kiss-Off." Their slogan: "Lips unite for civil rights."

The protest, which had an exceptionally large turnout, was held in the hallway outside the principal's office following sixth period on Thursday afternoon. Although instigators Salinger and Thompson reportedly fled the scene before the Kiss-Off could get underway, dozens of defiant students locked lips in Ms. Stickley's presence. The principal promptly announced another assembly, scheduled for Friday morning, to address the issue.

Apparently the Kiss-Off was a success, as it resulted in an about-face by Ms. Stickley, although instigators Thompson and Salinger were sentenced to a week of eraser-cleaning. On Friday, the principal retracted the No-Kissing rule, stating, "I have belatedly realized that my first responsibility is as an educator, not a chaperone. While fondling and petting will not be tolerated on campus, kissing will be permitted, as long as it does not cross the boundaries into bad taste."

Asked how he feels about the reversal, a victorious Justin Thompson commented, with a gleam in his eye, "Julia and I fully plan to take full advantage of the new policy."

Julia Salinger could not be reached for comment.

JULIA
I just wanted to tell you I'm... sorry. you know. About you and Erica.

GRIFFIN
Yeah? Why?

JULIA
Well... I just am. I mean, I know it's hard to break up with somebody, and since you're my... friend, I'm just sorry you have to go through that. You know?... But...it's okay if you don't want to talk about it.

GRIFFIN
What's to talk about?

JULIA
Oh. So...you broke up with her...? And not the other way around, I mean?

GRIFFIN
It just sorta happened. It's like, she was always talking. About nothing. You know?

JULIA
Yeah.

GRIFFIN
Anyway. See you around... Oh, yeah. Good luck with the kissing thing.

CLAUDIA

How could they do this?

JULIA

Like they couldn't even bother to stop and think that maybe this matters to us. This is—I mean, it's not like, hey, we're going to the grocery store, do you want to come with us? It's our brother's *wedding!*

BAILEY

You'd think—at least—at the very least—they could have been honest with us. What would that have cost them? I swear, nobody is ever straight with anybody anymore.

CLAUDIA

Well, see if I ever talk to them again.

JULIA

Claudia—

CLAUDIA

Forget it, I'm not...I wanted to be there. To watch them say all that mushy stuff, and for me to play "The Wedding March," and for us to throw rice...and maybe you'd catch the bouquet, Jul'... I wanted to watch them dance. I wanted to dance... It's always sad stuff—we're always together for the sad stuff. But *one time*, why couldn't we be together for something happy?

Hey, Everyone—

Sorry to break it to you this way, but Kirsten and I decided not to go with a big wedding after all. We flew to Reno instead. Make sure you look out for Owen while we're gone. We'll try and be back in time for the engagement party tomorrow night.

Charlie

Dinner Specials
Salinger's Restaurant
Friday, October 27, 1995

Appetizers
Jalapeño/Cream Cheese Poppers————————— $2.95
Blooming Onion————————————————————— $3.95

Soups Du Jour
Blue Corn Chowder————————cup, $1.50/bowl,$2.95
Baked French Onion in crock————————————— $3.50

Entrees
Blackened Spare Ribs
served with cajun rice and black beans————— $8.95

Herb-roasted Cornish game hens
served with garlic mashed potatoes and baby peas——— $10.95

Baked Salmon
served with rice pilaf and grilled vegetables———— $10.95

Burger Du Jour
1/4 Pound Ground Sirloin
served with smoked mozzarella, tomato, and onion——— $6.95

Pastas
Fusilli with olive oil, plum tomatoes,
garlic, and basil————————————————————— $7.50

Ziti with eggplant,
porcino mushrooms, and olives in marinara sauce——— $9.95

Salads
Smoked Chicken Caesar————————————————— $7.95
Spinach with warm bacon dressing—————————— $6.50

Desserts
Raspberry Sorbet with Chocolate Biscotti————— $2.50
Apple Tart a la mode————————————————————— $3.95
Chocolate Roulade with fudge sauce and whipped cream——— $3.95

CHARLIE
What are you gonna do, Joe? Are we gonna turn this place over to a total stranger?

JOE
I can't let you do this, Charlie. You've got things you wanna do with your life.

CHARLIE
Yeah, I know... So I won't paint houses anymore. I can probably live with that.

JOE
What about building furniture?

CHARLIE
Hey, I'm not giving that up! Forget it! I'm way too good at that. So I'll build some stuff for the restaurant. It'll be like my own private gallery. It might work out pretty good... What are you looking at me like that for? Give me a little support, will ya, Joe. This is kind of a momentous decision here.

JOE
Right.

CHARLIE
I don't know—I made so much noise for so long about how I *hated* this place. Could be there was some stupid little voice inside of me I just didn't wanna hear. You know—saying, hey, you could do worse—you could do way worse than Salinger's.

PAGE THREE

HAMPSHIRE COL
APPLICATION FOR A

(Essay Questions, Continued)

2. Discuss someone who has inspired you in one hundred and fifty words or less.

When someone is gone from your life for a really long time you start to forget stuff about them. Like you forget what their voice sounded like. Or how they loved you so much, and how everything you did was completely okay with them. And how that meant, in a weird way, that you could actually do kind of amazing things.

I'm not a very good student, and applying to college isn't so easy for me. So right now, what I am doing is I'm trying very hard to remember my mother's voice. I'm trying to remember it. Because I really need to hear it now. I'm listening for her to say to me what she always used to say... "Anything's possible, Bailey... Anything."

BAILEY
So, listen. I'm thinking I'm not gonna take my SATs again.

CHARLIE
How'd you do?

BAILEY
Nine hundred. Combined.

CHARLIE
I think that's about what I did... Yeah, so you took it. Don't put yourself through that stress again, man. Who needs it?

BAILEY
So, that's it, huh? You're not gonna give me a hard time?

CHARLIE
Nah.

BAILEY
Hey, Char, when you dropped outta school? Did anyone, like, try to talk you out of it?

CHARLIE
Are you kidding, man? You could hear Dad yelling from across the bridge... It was like he was always expecting me to disappoint him—and dropping out was just one more item on the checklist... But Mom...Mom knew the Berkeley thing was just about me running scared. So she left me alone for a couple months and then...I dunno how she said it.

BAILEY
Did what? I mean—

CHARLIE
—I was gonna re-enroll for the spring semester when the accident happened... Mom. She had that complete faith thing going. Remember?

MISS CORSO

First of all, you can relax already about the marriage... It's a good match. A very good match... Although, I can see why you'd worry. He was a scoundrel, this one.

KIRSTEN

Before he knew me.

MISS CORSO

And during. Let's be honest.

KIRSTEN

Okay. And during.

MISS CORSO

Well, he's got it out of his system for good. Oh, yes. Yes Yes Yes. I see the two of you, dancing at your wedding, with the love of a lifetime in your eyes.

KIRSTEN

Dancing. Huh. He doesn't really dance.

MISS CORSO

Well, he will. Both of you, like Astaire and what's-her-name. Oh, yes, you and Rob are going to have a long and happy life together.

KIRSTEN

Charlie.

MISS CORSO

Excuse me?

KIRSTEN

His name is Charlie.

MISS CORSO

No, it's not. I'm seeing it here, plain as day. Rob. R-O-B, Rob.

Miss Corso:
The San Francisco Psychic

This certificate entitles _Mr. Charlie Salinger and Ms. Kirsten Bennett_
to one free reading by the famed **Miss Corso.**
This certificate is non-transferable and expires one month from date of issue.
Presented by: _Aunt Roberta with love and best wishes for your upcoming wedding!_

On: _October 20 1995_

Miss Corso sees all, knows all

Non-transferable

Esmerelda Corso, Psychic
129 Union Street
San Francisco, California

...es:

...e rumor that's been going
...ot running for the office of Vice President of the Senior Class because anybody talked me into it, or because I need something impressive to put on my transcripts and college applications.

No, I'm running because I truly care about you, the students of Grant High School. I want to support you. I want to make a difference during this, our last year together.

I may not have straight-A's or a political track record, but I assure you that I'm the best man for the job. I won't make promises that I can't keep—like getting Soul Asylum to play at the prom or changing the academic schedule to allow half-days on Fridays. But I will do my best to listen to what you want, and make sure your voices are heard.

So vote for me, Bailey Salinger. I won't let you down. Thank you.

BAILEY
We're cool, right? Will's gonna take over, so you don't have to do any more work, and—

SARAH
Would you please shut up about the election.

BAILEY
Why? What's going on with you?

SARAH
What the hell, I have like zero self-respect left anyway. Do you actually think I was doing this because I'm so civic-minded? Because I *care* who governs the student body? Or that it matters to me whether it's me or Will who hangs your posters in the halls? I did this because I'm in love with you, you jerk. Feel free not to say anything.

KIRSTEN

I'm scared.

CHARLIE

Because I leave junk mail on the counter...?

KIRSTEN

No, because I know you're in love with me and you're willing to overlook things right now. But I have this...little problem, Charlie. I can't have children and...I know you say you're okay with it now, but I've been here. I've watched you go through this whole thing. And I'm scared because I saw your face when I found out Spencer wasn't really your son. And I saw how much it mattered to you. Your heart is broken over something you want *so bad* and...I can never, ever give you. And I don't want you to just say you're okay with that now and then wake up in a few years and realize you're not...

CHARLIE

I won't do that...

KIRSTEN

You might, Charlie. We're looking at an entire lifetime together. With no children of our own and...I can live with all these little piles of paper on the counter...I *can*...but...Can you honestly tell me you're okay with that? Can you?

Please share our joy and happiness as we,

Charles Salinger

and

Kirsten Bennett

are joined in marriage on Saturday, the eighteenth of November Nineteen hundred and ninety-five at Two O'clock in the afternoon The Salinger Residence 3324 Broadway San Francisco, California

Reception to follow

Julia,

Now that a few days have passed since— well, you know, Saturday night— I was wondering how you were feeling about what happened. I mean, I know how I feel. Great. I feel totally great. I have no— I was kind of hoping you were feeling the same way, now. Because everything you said about waiting for the right time, and the right person— well, Julia, as far as I'm concerned, it was the right time and you were— are— always will be— the right person for me. And it couldn't have been any more meaningful or beautiful if it had happened in some really romantic place, or on our wedding night, or after months of planning and waiting. It was perfect, and I hope you see it that way, too. I think we need to talk about it, though. Or maybe we don't. Maybe we should just go on from here. Take things as they come. What do you think? My parents are going out tonight, and they won't be back until late. I was thinking maybe you could come over. We don't have to do anything. Or, if you want to, we could. I mean, what I'm trying to say is that it's totally up to you. I'll be waiting by your locker after school.

Love,
Justin

JULIA

You know, I... I don't know... It's like I don't know whether to be really pissed off at you, or to apologize.

JUSTIN

It doesn't have to be someone's fault, you know...or even...even a mistake...

JULIA

No, right. Stuff just *happens*. You get married, or you don't. You save yourself for when it's special, or you get really drunk and just *do* it... Same difference, right?

JUSTIN

...No. Of course not.

JULIA

I want it to be special. And that means with *some-one* special. I mean, it doesn't *have* to be the one person ever. But *it'd be nice*... I mean it'd be nice... right after it happens... to look at that other person and say—you *could* be the one... Or at least a friend. At least someone you love. And who feels kinda the same way... about you... Then it'd be okay. Then it'd be nice.

Charles Salinger and Kirsten Bennett

regret to announce

that their wedding, scheduled for November 18, 1995,

did not take place.

Your kind gift is herewith returned,

along with heartfelt gratitude

for your thoughtfulness and generosity.

KIRSTEN
I would have given you everything I have today—God, Charlie, I would have given you *me*. I can't give you more than that. I don't know how... If that's not enough. If you're not sure—

CHARLIE
—I'm sure. *I'm sure.*

KIRSTEN
No! You're not, Charlie. And I'm sorry—but some things you say you just can't take back. The most honest thing you said today was—I don't want to get married.

CHARLIE
So—maybe I made a mistake. Please don't do this to me, Kirsten. *Please.*

KIRSTEN
What do you want me to do? I don't have a choice. I'm afraid to marry you. I'm afraid of the day you'll come into our bedroom and say—I don't want you anymore.

CHARLIE
I won't say that.

KIRSTEN
I don't believe you! I love you—but I don't believe you—and I can't take the chance. Cause I would die, Charlie... So I'm gonna walk away from you. And from these children...who I love...

JULIA
She can't just *quit*! I mean, she's too good to just quit.

BAILEY
Yeah, well, what if that's what she really wants?

JULIA
She's too young to know what she really wants.

ROSS
You don't spend years of your life working that hard, becoming that good, just to throw it all away.

CHARLIE
Maybe it's that Jody girl she's been hanging with— Maybe she has something to do with it.

BAILEY
Maybe she's just had enough. And if she doesn't want to play anymore, isn't that, like, *her* business? Why is this up for a vote?

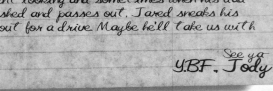

Hey, Claud—

Im sitting here in Social Studies pretending to be taking notes like a good little student. Meanwhile, I came up with the following list of things we can do after school— you are still planning to bag the violin lesson, right?

1. Go over to Salinger's so you can snag some more cigs and another bottle of rum from behind the bar, then go home to your tent and get wasted.

2. Sneak into the new Brad Pitt movie at the matinee over at the Multiplex— you can distract that ditzy red-haired ticket girl by pretending you're some foreign tourist asking for directions while I get in. I'll go plug the sinks and toilets and start a flood in the ladies' room, then I'll yell to the ticket girl that there's an emergency situation so you can sneak in.

3. Go hide out in the janitor's closet next to the boys' locker room so we can look through the crack in the wall and check out the soccer team taking showers after practice.

What do you think? Let me know before last period. Oh, and by the way, you should give me your locker combo so I don't have to keep shoving these notes through the vents. The other day, one got jammed there and I broke a pen trying to push it in anyway. I figured I could keep some stuff in your locker cuz it's closer to my classes than mine is. Okay?

Oh by the way, Jared McDonald asked me why we've been hanging out with Fiddle Girl and I told him you decided to drop out of dorkestra and that you're actually pretty cool. He, like, couldn't believe it. I think he likes you, but he was probably thinking you were some music nerd. Now who knows what might happen? Do you like him? He and I used to be pretty tight but he's had an attitude problem ever since he got out of rehab but he's still semi-decent-looking and sometimes when his dad gets trashed and passes out, Jared sneaks his Porsche out for a drive. Maybe he'll take us with him!

See ya
Y.B.F. Jody

APPLICATION FOR ENROLLMENT
THE WEE SCHOOL Pre-school

NAME: Owen Salinger

DOB: June 14, 1993

ADDRESS: 332A Broadway
San Francisco, California

TELEPHONE: 555-782A

FATHER: Charlie Salinger (brother & legal guardian)

MOTHER: Deceased

PARENT'S EMPLOYMENT: Manager, Salinger's Restaurant

WORK PHONE: 555-3663

ALLERGIES? Not that I'm aware of

POTTY TRAINED? ~~No~~ Yes (Although he does have an occasional accident)

EMERGENCY CONTACT: Kirsten Bennett

DAYTIME PHONE: 555-9433

RELATIONSHIP: ~~Frien~~ ~~Family friend~~ Former Nanny

WHY DO YOU WANT YOUR CHILD TO ATTEND THE WEE SCHOOL?
I feel that of all the pre-schools in San Francisco, the Wee School is the best ~~because it is~~ for various reasons too lengthy and numerous to list here. Also, it is conveniently located, and Owen needs to be around other children his age.

CHARLIE
When can he start?
TEACHER CAROL
Well—there are a few little issues we have to deal with first.
CHARLIE
Of course. You probably want a deposit, right—
TEACHER CAROL
—Yes—
CHARLIE
And this is for five days a week, right?
TEACHER CAROL
Yes. But, Mr. Salinger, we require the child to come in and meet with us for a few minutes first.
CHARLIE
Okay, sure.
TEACHER CAROL
Good. We can schedule it for... day after tomorrow? And one more thing. We do require that all our children be completely potty-trained before they begin.
CHARLIE
...Not...a problem! That's not a problem. He practically poops on demand... Can we make that appointment late in the day?

Bailey's Real Hot Chocolate

Ingredients

1 cup boiling water
1/4 cup cocoa
1/8 teaspoon salt
4 tablespoons sugar
1/2 teaspoon cinnamon
3 cups scalded milk
1 teaspoon vanilla

Combine over low heat: boiling water, cocoa, salt, sugar, and cinnamon. Stir continuously for two minutes until ingredients are blended well. Add scalded milk and heat through. Using wire whisk, beat in vanilla just before serving.

Serves four children, or two adults (or one teenage boy)

Dear Charlie, Bailey, Julia, Claudia & Owen:

This isn't easy— but then, it's never easy to say good-bye. Not now, to the five grandchildren I never knew I had. And not thirty years ago, to the daughter I desperately wanted to see grow up.

I'm not going to try and explain why I left my wife and child— because I was a different person back then, and I have no idea what I was thinking. Anyway, even if I did understand why I left, it's too late for explanations. I'll never be able to change what I did, and what I lost.

I know that your mother could never have forgiven me for not being there on her birthdays or at her violin recitals. Or on the day she married your father. Or on the days when each of you was born. I know how many precious moments I've missed. That's why I came back to San Francisco: to find your mother and beg her to forgive me, so that I could be part of her life if she'd let me. I never expected to find out Diana was dead— or that she had left behind five beautiful children, each of whom reminded me, in some way, of my little girl.

But I can understand why you won't forgive me. Why should you? And why should she have forgiven me? Like I said, she wouldn't have. She was stubborn, your mother. And she expected a lot from people. She deserved far more than I ever gave her. I'm glad to see that she found, in your father and in all of you, the love she needed so badly from me.

I wish I hadn't waited so long to realize I needed my daughter and her family in my life. But that isn't going to happen, and I can't say I blame you for not wanting to welcome an old man who's offering too little, too late. I want you to know that you don't have to worry about me popping in again to complicate your lives. I promise to leave you alone from now on. But if you ever need anything— just call and I'll be there.

With love,

Grandpa Jake

JAKE
Julia—we're family.

JULIA
I don't care—

JAKE
—And we don't have that many people besides each other.

JULIA
I don't care.

JAKE
But someday you may. I'm telling you, someday you may care very much. And it may be too late. And you never know when it's going to be. So you have to avoid it...at all costs. At all costs you have to avoid being too late.

JULIA
You waited thirty years. I don't feel sorry for you... I feel sorry for her. And I feel sorry for me, cause I should have had a grandfather.

JAKE
I wanna try. I wanna try with you. Because you are...you are *so much* like her. Julia—You are you're mother—standing there. And you are the closest I'm ever going to come to seeing even a hint of her again.

CHARLIE

I liked to draw skyscrapers when I was little. I made this picture once, and I brought it in to show Dad, and he looked at it, and kinda sat me on his lap and I remember thinking he was going to hug me, and instead, he started going on about proportions. How it needed to be wider at the base. How a building that tall and narrow would just fall right over. God, I hated that—his...argh...his insane expectations. Now, all of a sudden, it turns out—I've got 'em too. I'm making the same mistakes. His mistakes. Go figure, huh?

CLAUDIA

God, that's so weird. He wasn't ever like that with me.

CHARLIE

Huh. Maybe that's the way it happens. With parents and firstborns. I guess by the time the other kids come, they've learned not to push so hard... Owen— he's Dad's last, but he's kinda my *first*, you know? So, I was thinking... I should clear a space on the wall for this. Frame it. So he knows. It didn't need windows.

JULIA
I'm sorry. I'm sorry. I just feel so...sad, you know?

JUSTIN
Yeah. But the fact that it happened the way it did—I mean, for me—there's this tiny, tiny relief. It makes it easier, doesn't it?

JULIA
Not much. No, actually.

JUSTIN
You didn't do anything, Jul.

JULIA
But I can't really act like the choice was taken out of my hands. Because I would've *made* the choice, Justin. It was, like, the least worst of a lot of bad options and I would have done it... But you know what? Any way it happens—*any* way—it's still hard.

Dear Justin:

I know you want to be there for me now, and that you think we should work through this together, because it happened to both of us. But— and I don't mean this in any way that diminishes your involvement or how much you care, because I know you do— it happened to <u>me</u>. Not to you or to us. It was my body, and it was my choice, and even though in the end I wasn't forced to go through with it, I have come to terms with what happened. And I need some space to do that, Justin.

I keep thinking about how, when I lost my parents, people would come fluttering around, asking if I wanted to talk, if there was anything they could do. And even though I wanted to say yes, even though I wanted there to be something someone could do to help me get over it— in the end, there was nothing. The only thing that helped was time. So that's what I need from you, Justin. Just time. I hope you understand.

Julia

February 27, 1996

Dear Julia,

I know I said when I left I probably wouldn't write, but I figure you know by now that I do a lot of things that I don't plan to do. So here I am, at MILITARY SCHOOL with the GOOD OL' BOYS, just where my father wanted me to be. According to him, I'm LUCKY— this is supposed to be better than going to PRISON— which is where I should be— for stealing money from that guy's jacket at your restaurant. But I'm not so sure. To me, it's the SAME THING. And if I were in prison in California, at least you'd be close by so you could visit me.

BUT MAYBE YOU WOULDN'T. You probably wouldn't, since you're back together with Justin. Not that I blame you. I didn't expect you to WAIT AROUND FOREVER WHILE I PAY THE PRICE FOR THE STUPID THING I DID. I just want you to know that. Anyway, Louisiana's beautiful, but the REDNECK MUSIC SUCKS and so does THIS PLACE. I hope you're happy, and that you'll find time to write me back. I'LL UNDERSTAND IF YOU DON'T. But I wanted you to know that I'm thinking about you. And I miss you. And if I could take back what I did, and go back to the way things were with you— I WOULD.

GRIFFIN

GRIFFIN
So I guess you got pregnant, huh?

JULIA
You could tell?

GRIFFIN
No, I just figured. You know...what else could it be?

JULIA
Oh. I'm not pregnant now. I lost it. I mean—a miscarriage... But I almost had an abortion.

GRIFFIN
Whoa... Are you okay? I mean, physically?

JULIA
Yeah, I'm okay.

GRIFFIN
Good. Was he cool about it?

JULIA
Yeah. Very.

GRIFFIN
So how come you're here?

JULIA
I don't know. Maybe I thought you'd under-stand.

CHARLIE

The restaurant's doing great.

KATHLEEN

Yes, it is. I'd like to think I had something to do with that.

CHARLIE

You did. A lot.

KATHLEEN

I've been thinking about that, actually—just because you and I aren't together anymore, that doesn't mean I should give up something I put so much time and energy and money into.

CHARLIE

Kathleen, what're you—?

KATHLEEN

I've put together an investment group. We're buying the whole building... I know it's a good location for a restaurant. Not necessarily *your* restaurant—

CHARLIE

What?

KATHLEEN

If I were you, I wouldn't expect my lease to be renewed.

REINVENTING A CLASSIC

BY STEPHEN GIEGEN-MILLER
FOOD CRITIC

Bustling, noisy, and friendly, Salinger's has been a Union Street fixture for over two decades.

A true gourmand wouldn't have given the original menu a second look, but it was chock-full of relatively tasty, all-American crowd-pleasers, from cheeseburgers to tortellini. And with its ceiling fans and exposed brick, easygoing staff and well-stocked bar, this laid-back restaurant has always been perfect for a breezy first date or a noisy family celebration.

It still is.

But the no-surprises menu has recently been replaced by a sublime array of delicacies reflecting the best of Mexican, Oriental, and Italian cuisine with a unique American flair. And for that, we have manager Charlie Salinger to thank.

The restaurant, now owned by Joe Mangus, was originally managed by Salinger's father, Nick. After the senior Salinger and his wife, Diana, were killed in a tragic automobile accident two years ago, their eldest son not only took over the responsibility of raising his four younger siblings—the youngest of whom is two—but he also wound up at the helm of his father's establishment.

Despite his age (twenty-five) and his appearance (shaggy-haired and rumpled, with a devil-may-care swagger), no one who dines in the renovated Salinger's would think to call Charlie Salinger a slacker. He has, in the past month, transformed his late father's business into a divine eatery.

His first coup? Wooing chef artiste Terrell Moore away from his longtime post at Entre Nous. Moore, known in epicurean circles for his classic French cuisine, has displayed an impressive creative capacity in his latest dishes, from the oversized appetizers to the decadent desserts.

Another feat: the revamped wine list is suitable for both the budget-conscious patron and the discriminating connoisseur. The comprehensive selection contains intriguing local and foreign offerings, culminating in the outrageously expensive, thoroughly impressive limited production Moet & Chandon Dom Perignon Rosé Champagne.

As a prelude to dinner, I was promptly and cheerfully presented with a heaping basket of fresh baked breads, featuring a nicely tangy sourdough loaf and crusty, piping-hot dill rolls. The basket was thoughtfully accompanied by a ramekin of whipped butter and a cruet of herbed virgin olive oil.

The
bisque
charm
served
pale pi
shell-li
bowl, w
electric
flavor. I
next intr
by an u
offering
sweet-an
herring
canapes,

Justin Thompson
English
Section Three
Folk Tale Assignment

THE WEED

(Second Draft)

Once, there was a couple named Jersey and Geraldine. They'd been together so long, they could barely remember a time when they weren't. But they remembered the moment they fell in love, because even though it was a long time ago, it felt like yesterday to them. Or at least, yesterday it felt like yesterday. Because today, they had started to drift apart. And Geraldine knew it was all their house's fault. Because the old place was full of problems, like cracks that let in cold air during the winter, and pipes that were so squeaky they played the *Twilight Zone* theme every night. So they decided it was time they move away.

So Jersey and Geraldine started packing away their old things. And it was good to get rid of what they didn't need. There was the head of the Unicorn he had killed to impress her, not knowing it was her favorite flying horse. The broken piece of looking glass that she used to put on makeup—which he said she never needed. But when they checked under their bed to make sure they'd packed everything, they found something strange. There behind the missing socks, a thick, ugly weed was growing. And they knew from its size that it must have been there a while.

They yanked at the weed, they hacked and burned it, they even tried feeding it Jersey's worst borscht, the one that killed Uncle Traugott. But every time, the weed came back, even stronger than before.

Geraldine and Jersey were old and wise, but there was somebody in their land who was wiser—and plenty older. Some people thought she was ugly. Others thought the warts gave her character. But everybody knew the Answer Hag lived up to her name.

Answer Hag told Geraldine and Jersey if there was any magic that could solve their weed problem, it wasn't something she could give them. It was something they already had—or used to have—and it was right under their noses. Something bigger than an air kiss, but smaller than the LA-Z-Boy she made him throw away. And they wouldn't know what it was until it came along and bit them.

So Geraldine and Jersey searched everywhere for the thing that was missing. Was it the ancient shoes he wore to their wedding? Was it the lock of her hair that she gave him when they were engaged? It was none of these. And then one day, while they searched the house separately, Geraldine and Jersey met in a hallway and couldn't get by. But when he moved left, she moved right. And when she moved left, he moved right. And pretty soon they realized they were dancing. And it made them laugh. And when they laughed they heard the house shake with a strange noise. Almost like it was laughing with them. They went downstairs and saw that the noise was the giant weed getting sucked through the floor, like inhaled back into the earth. And the more they laughed, the faster the weed went away.

As the couple danced into the dark cold night, their house just got warmer and brighter. And they knew that no other house could keep them as close. So they unpacked their bags to stay. And they lived happily ever after.

JUSTIN
So? Did you read it?

JULIA
Uh-huh. Just finished...

JUSTIN
So that's all you're gonna say? That you finished it?

JULIA
I liked it. I thought it was good.

JUSTIN
Why don't I believe you?

JULIA
I didn't say I didn't have any problems.

JUSTIN
Okay. Problems. That's why I gave it to you. To hear your problems. So hurt me. I'm ready.

JULIA
Well... I liked the stuff with the weed. I think it's a good, you know, symbol or whatever. But the way they got rid of it... I mean, they accidentally find this potion that magically makes it go away? Can't you do better than that?

BAILEY

—So, wait a minute. Now Saturday's out, too?

SARAH

Yeah. We just...got this call from a girl at Central High and the lead singer of the band who was supposed to play their spring dance came down with mono or something so they needed a replacement and we needed the gig so...Matt booked it. I'm sorry.

BAILEY

No, no. You shouldn't be sorry. You guys are taking off and that's...

SARAH

Pretty cool, huh? Oh, I can't meet you for lunch—I gotta xerox some sheet music—so I'll just see you between classes, okay?

BAILEY

And after school.

SARAH

Rehearsal. But you're coming tonight, right? I mean, I know it's just the coffee-house *again* but we can hang out between sets... **BAILEY**

Um, actually... I'm starting to feel a little like Yoko Ono, so I was thinking I might just... catch a movie with Will.

LIVE MUSIC
Salinger's Restaurant

proudly presents
the popular San Francisco band

NIELSON FAMILY

featuring new vocalist Sarah Reeves
10:30 Friday Night

Five Dolla

Bailey—
I know you said you might have to watch Owen on Friday night but I know Julia would cover for you so that you could come and watch us. It would really mean a lot to me to have you there
—Sarah

KIRSTEN

You only want me because you can't have me, Charlie. You're afraid of losing me.

CHARLIE

Yeah, I am. Because I love you. And I think—I think—if you love me—I think we could be happy together. So...do you? Love me?

KIRSTEN

I'm getting married, Charlie.

CHARLIE

That's not an answer.

KIRSTEN

You love me.

CHARLIE

Yes.

KIRSTEN

You're ready for all the things you weren't ready for six months ago.

CHARLIE

I am.

KIRSTEN

And you think *I'm* kidding myself? Ask yourself this, Charlie: Would you be doing any of this— feeling this way, wanting me so much— if you weren't watching everything else in your life go down the drain?

Salinger's Restaurant to close

BY NADINE WETTLAUFER
COMMUNITY REPORTER

Joe Mangus, owner of the recently revamped Salinger's Restaurant on Union Street, has announced that the establishment will shut down at the end of this month.

"We've lost our lease," he stated tersely when asked why he has chosen to go out of business at the height of his restaurant's success.

Salinger's is housed in a building that was recently purchased by the newly formed Eisley Financial Group. Kathleen Eisley, a local television news producer and a recent recipient of the Bay Area TV News award for Best Investigative Series, is chairman and spokesperson for the investment group.

"We agree that the building is a fine location for a restaurant, but we have something far more upscale than Salinger's in mind. We regret any inconvenience this has caused to the management and patrons of Salinger's. We are looking toward the future, and are currently going over blueprints of the building with designers from Los Angeles in anticipation of making some much-needed aesthetic changes as soon as Salinger's vacates the premises."

Charlie Salinger, manager of Salinger's, declined to comment for this article.

BAILEY
I'm not going away to school... It's a done deal. I'm using my scholarship money to keep the restaurant open. It's complicated— Jake worked out the details.

SARAH
I don't get it. I thought getting out of here was the most important thing to you.

BAILEY
I thought so too. But, see...the problem is... I've spent two years fighting, *really fighting* to keep us all together. So the idea... that I would be the first to leave... I mean, us being a family no matter what...that was... that was the whole point. And *you*. You're the whole point.

SARAH
Bailey—

BAILEY
—And I don't like what happened to me. It's like for a second there, it all just felt like too much. And I couldn't handle it. But the thing is—I have to handle it... Because being with you, and taking care of them...that's kinda who I am.

BAILEY

Look, are you happy? Are you, Sarah? Do I make you happy anymore? Cause I don't think I do.

SARAH

Sure you do. Of course you do... I don't make *you* happy, is that what you're really saying? Is it?

BAILEY

Not a whole helluva lot makes me happy these days.

SARAH

Including me. Say it. Just say it. Please.

BAILEY

Okay—including you.

SARAH

So what do we do about that? How do we fix that?

BAILEY

We don't. Sarah, when it's bad almost all the time and you need to change so much to make the other person okay, that you're not even yourself anymore—that's when people break up.

SARAH

You want to break up?

BAILEY

It's not working. Us. When it stops being good is when it should be over... So, yeah. Yes. I do.

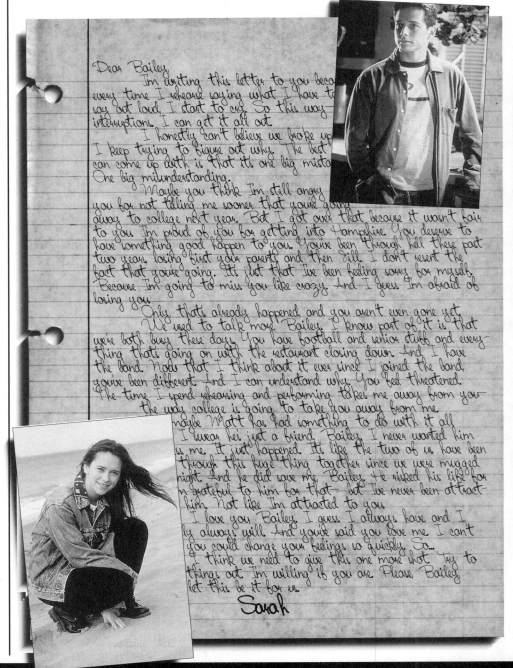

June 1, 1996

Dear Griffin,

By now you must be almost finished with school for the year and ma[k]-
ing plans for the summer. I guess you[...]
not coming home to San Francisco, h[uh?]
I mean, if you were, you probably wou[ld]
have let me know by now. Anyway, I[...]
hope whatever you have planned will [be]
fun. Maybe you're staying there in L[...]
school. Or maybe you're going off to Europe [...]
God, wouldn't *that* be great?

As for me, I'm not sure exactly what I'm going
to do. I'm not really looking forward to having so much
time on my hands. As I wrote in my last letter,
Justin and I broke up last month. It's been really
hard getting used to being without him. I mean, We
were together for over a year, and before that, we were
friends since we were babies. So it's like I keep expecting it to be him when the phone rings, and I have to
stop myself from dropping in when I drive past his
house. But I suppose it'll get easier. That's what
everybody says, anyway.

I applied for a summer internship at this publishing house down near the wharf. You know how I've
always been interested in writing and editorial work.
it sounds perfect for me. So I'm crossing my fingers,
hoping I get it. After all, it would keep me busy and
take my mind off things, at least for a while.

I hope you're well, Griffin. Write back if you want
to. I'll be around.

Sincerely,
Julia

JULIA

I don't know what you want from me.

GRIFFIN

What are you talking about? I'm in love with you.

JULIA

Come on, Griffin—!

GRIFFIN

That's like all I am, is in love with you.

JULIA

Then what are you doing? Are you playing games? Cause I don't understand. I really don't.

GRIFFIN

See, it's like, this afternoon, after we talked, I was...*happy*. You know? Like *really happy*. I mean, you don't even know. And then I started to think about it—about us... And I kinda freaked.

JULIA

I don't—

GRIFFIN

—Cause it's like all this time there were all these things in our way. And now there's nothing. Now it's just—it's up to me. But what if I don't get it right this time? Then it's over. Then I have nothing...and I don't want to have nothing.

ELLIE

I hope you'll be happy. You and Kirsten.

CHARLIE

You do? Since when?

ELLIE

I'm sorry. About yesterday... I'm going to get off your back, Charlie. No more letters. No more insults. I promise.

CHARLIE

Great. That's just great, Ellie.

ELLIE

I thought that's what you wanted.

CHARLIE

I guess I'm kinda past the point of being grateful to you for not telling me what a loser I am.

ELLIE

Oh, for God's sake, Charlie, I didn't mean—

CHARLIE

—It's not good enough for you to just stop being negative, Ellie. What, then? What do you want?

ELLIE

What, then? What do you want?

CHARLIE

I want you to give me some credit. Actually say, "Yeh, Charlie, you've made mistakes, but you've turned things around, and you're doing okay, you're being responsible and I can see why she loves you." You know, the kinds of things kids need to hear from their parents. And since you're kinda the only parent around, it would've been nice if... Well, it just woulda been nice... But, I guess that's just the way it is.

August 27 1996

Dear Kirsten,

Since you refused to return yet another of my phone calls I am forced to put my feelings on paper once again I simply cannot sit by and watch you make this terrible mistake. I don't understand what you can possibly be thinking moving in with Charlie again after he left you at the alter. I can understand why you called off your wedding to Michael. It was just too soon you were on the rebound you loved his child. But you seem to have followed a very good level-headed decision with the worst choice you have ever made. You will never be able to trust Charlie after what he did to you. He ruined your life once— can't you see its going to happen again? You don't belong in San Francisco anymore in that house with those children and him. We are your family. Come back home to Chicago Kirsten. Your father and I will help ... call to discuss this. I'll be ... to hear from you...

Fondly
Mother

JULIA
You're back! Poison Ivy? Poison Oak?

CLAUDIA
I'm clean. Hey, Jul, guess what—

CHARLIE
Wait a sec. Have you—did you—?

CLAUDIA
Two inches. Anyway, the thing is, I met—

BAILEY
Are we cutting into this cake, cause I skipped lunch.

KIRSTEN
I told you you'd have a good time, didn't I? And you didn't believe me.

CLAUDIA
I met a boy and fell in love, okay? I'm in love... Just thought you'd want to know.

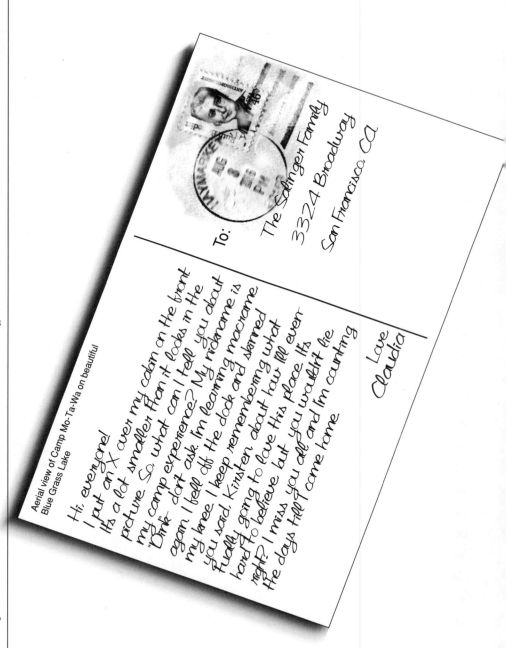

Aerial view of Camp Mo-Ta-Wa on beautiful Blue Grass Lake

TO:
The Salinger Family
3324 Broadway
San Francisco, CA

Hi, everyone!
I put an X over my cabin on the front. It's a lot smaller than it looks in the picture. So, what can I tell you about my camp experience? My nickname is "Dirk"— don't ask. I'm learning macrame again. I fell off the dock and skinned my knee. I keep remembering what you said. Kirsten about how 100 even finally going to love this place. It's hard to believe but you wouldn't lie right? I miss you all and I'm counting the days till I come home

Love
Claudia

Julia's Spicy Eggplant Stew

<u>Ingredients</u>

Olive oil
2 large firm eggplants
1 medium onion, chopped
2 cloves garlic, minced
1 cup sliced fresh mushrooms
6 fresh tomatoes, coarsely chopped
1/4 cup minced fresh basil leaves
1/4 cup minced fresh oregano leaves
1 fifteen-ounce can of tomato sauce
Dried hot pepper flakes
Salt
4 cups cooked, drained short pasta (such as
rotini, fusilli or shells)

Cut eggplant into bitesized chunks. Fill bottom
of large frying pan with approximately 1/2
cup olive oil and place over medium heat.
Sauté eggplant, onion, and garlic, adding more
oil as needed to prevent sticking. When egg
plant is browned and onion is nearly trans
parent, add mushrooms, tomatoes, basil, oregano,
tomato sauce, pepper flakes, and salt to taste.
Simmer one hour or longer over low heat. Serve
hot or cold. Makes four mealsized portions or
eight appetizer/side dish portions.

GRIFFIN
I've been thinking about what you said, you know? About me needing things in my life that matter. Besides you.

JULIA
I never said anything about *leaving*. I thought we were gonna figure this out together. And now you're just...running away...

GRIFFIN
I'm coming back. That's the whole point. I just—everything's screwy with us right now, you know? And that's kinda my fault. I mean, you're starting to hate me—

JULIA
I don't hate you...

GRIFFIN
You know what I mean. And that's exactly what I was scared of. That I was gonna screw this up. And if I keep hanging around here, I'm only gonna make it worse so... it's sorta up to me. I gotta do something about that. About *me*. S'at make sense?

JULIA
I don't want you to go.

GRIFFIN
I don't want to go.

JULIA
We do this a lot, huh? Say good-bye.

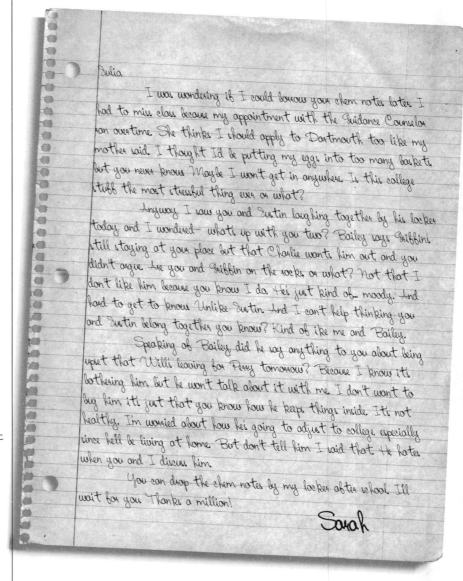

Julia,

I was wondering if I could borrow your chem notes later. I had to miss class because my appointment with the Guidance Counselor ran overtime. She thinks I should apply to Dartmouth too like my mother said. I thought I'd be putting my eggs into too many baskets but you never know. Maybe I won't get in anywhere. Is this college stuff the most stressful thing ever or what?

Anyway, I saw you and Justin laughing together by his locker today and I wondered— what's up with you two? Bailey says Griffin's still staying at your place but that Charlie wants him out and you didn't argue. Are you and Griffin on the rocks or what? Not that I don't like him because you know I do. He's just kind of... moody. And hard to get to know. Unlike Justin. And I can't help thinking you and Justin belong together you know? Kind of like me and Bailey.

Speaking of Bailey, did he say anything to you about being upset that Will's leaving for Perry tomorrow? Because I know it's bothering him but he won't talk about it with me. I don't want to bug him it's just that you know how he keeps things inside. It's not healthy. I'm worried about how he's going to adjust to college especially since he'll be living at home. But don't tell him I said that. He hates when you and I discuss him.

You can drop the chem notes by my locker after school. I'll wait for you. Thanks a million!

Sarah

HOW TO SUCCEED IN COLLEGE WITHOUT REALLY TRYING

by Cooper Voight

1.   Don't take an Intro to Computers course. People who take this course have been known to commit suicide. Instead, take a proficiency test to excuse you from said course.

2.   Cheat on aforementioned computer proficiency test. This is easily accomplished. Simply find a willing and cash-short upperclassman who will take the test for you. This simply entails logging on in the computer lab using your social security number.

3.   Only buy used textbooks. Not only are they cheaper, but chances are, someone will already have highlighted anything you'd ever need to know.

4.   Eat free in the cafeteria without purchasing a meal plan. Simply find a willing friend who <u>has</u> a meal plan and is willing to share. He will, using the utmost charm, tell the cafeteria cashier he forgot his card today; she will then allow him to pass through the line without paying. You can then use his card as credit for your lunch.

5.   Avoid taking complicated science labs. Instead, register for Geology 101—otherwise known as "Rocks for Jocks." If you've got opposable thumbs, you're pretty much guaranteed a B.

6.   Avoid taking complicated English courses. Instead, register for Survey of Children's Literature. The reading list is compiled of short, easy books like "Charlotte's Web" and "The Pigman."

When in doubt, drink.

BAILEY
Hey, you know what—I oughta beat the crap out of you!... I guess you didn't think I'd find out what was going on with you and Julia.

COOPER
What? What did Julia—?

BAILEY
I'm telling you—You do anything—You...you *touch* her, you force her to do anything, *anything* she doesn't wanna do—

COOPER
—Get your finger out of my face—

BAILEY
—I'll kill you—!

COOPER
—GET IT OUT OF MY FACE OR I'LL BREAK IT OFF.

BAILEY
Like I'm scared. What—what is it—what do you do? Is it the—I'm a college guy. You wanna date a college guy you gotta put out. Is that the line?

COOPER
Is that what she told you?

BAILEY
She didn't need to. I'm finally figuring out what kind of guy you are.

BAILEY

I'm not moving in with Callie. I'm moving in with her *and her boyfriend*. They're a couple.

SARAH

Yeah? So why doesn't he keep her from walking around half-naked?

BAILEY

Cause it doesn't matter. I've seen attractive girls in underwear before. It's not a big deal.

SARAH

So you think she's attractive?

BAILEY

No. I mean, I don't know. Who cares? Maybe she is, maybe she isn't—

SARAH

She is.

BAILEY

Okay, fine. Let's say she is. Let's say she's off the charts gorgeous. *It doesn't matter*... I love you, Sarah. I'm probably more attracted to you than you want to know. I'm so attracted to you that if someone dropped Michelle Pfeiffer, naked, in my lap, all it would do is make me think of you.

SARAH

Really?

BAILEY

Really. So don't worry about Callie. Honestly. She's just some semi-insane girl who isn't you.

APARTME

MALE OR FEMALE wanted to share one-bedroom floor-through apartment with two roommates. Ten minute walk from campus. $215 per month.

n, living area, laundry

CLAUDIA

I can't believe you stole my boyfriend...

JULIA

What?! All right. First of all, that's...totally insane, okay? And second of all, if you wanna get mad at somebody, get mad at Byron.

CLAUDIA

I'm mad at both of you! I mean, you don't know what it's like to grow up in this stupid house with everybody's boyfriends and girlfriends always parading through here—

JULIA

Claudia. I'm sorry. But I didn't do anything...

CLAUDIA

Yes you did! I finally had my own boyfriend. It was finally *my* turn. And then *you* walked into the room with, with...your face on and all of a sudden he doesn't care about *me* anymore.

September 3, 1996

Dear Diary,

Something's going on with Byron. It's like, the whole time we were away at camp, he seemed crazy about me. But the minute we got back to San Francisco, he started acting I don't know, distant. Well, maybe not the minute we got back. Things were pretty normal at first. I guess he only started acting weird after he got to know my family. Namely, Julia. I could be wrong but it's almost like he kind of, well, likes her. Not in a liking your girlfriend's older sister way. More in a... girlfriend way. It's not fair. She's older and beautiful and experienced and smart and she's always hanging around the house, being Julia. How can I compete with someone like her? Besides, she and Griffin aren't doing that great these days. Ever since he got back from Thailand a few weeks ago, they've been arguing. Charlie says he can't stay here anymore and Julia's not even arguing with him about that. For all I know, she's in the market for a new man and Byron's right under her nose. He's so cute and witty, and he plays soccer and everything. If I don't do something Julia's going to steal him away from me. But I won't let that happen Diary. I, Claudia Salinger, am going to fight to keep my man!

PHOTO EXHIBITION!

"A Study in Nude"

by photographer *John Thompson*

featuring student model *Callie Martel*

Sunset Gallery
Wine and Cheese Opening
Saturday, September 21, 1996

4-7 p.m.

CALLIE
He's really a very talented photographer, don't you think?

BAILEY
Oh, very. *Very* talented... Stuffy in here, don't you think?

CALLIE
And his use of chiaroscuro! I mean, right over there, the way the light kinda spills over the edge of my thigh. That took a long time to get right.

BAILEY
Uh-huh. Someone should open a window... I had no idea you were so...so...

CALLIE
Uninhibited?

BAILEY
Limber. You're a very limber girl... Geez, you'd think they'd have air-conditioning.

CALLIE
Why don't I get us something to drink? Don't disappear on me.

CHARLIE
Why has Jody been hanging around here all the time? Why have you been there every day? And don't tell me she's having boyfriend troubles.

CLAUDIA
She, uh...she has this problem with her mom's boyfriend. He...he sorta kissed her. Nothing happened, but...

CHARLIE
What? And you kept this a secret? *Claudia!*

CLAUDIA
Well...she asked me to. Her mom's practically gonna marry this guy. Jody doesn't know what to do. So maybe if she has a little time to figure this out—What are you doing? You can't call her mom. Charlie! What do I tell Jody—?

CHARLIE
—SI'DOWN!... Hello? Mrs. Lynch? This is Charlie Salinger.

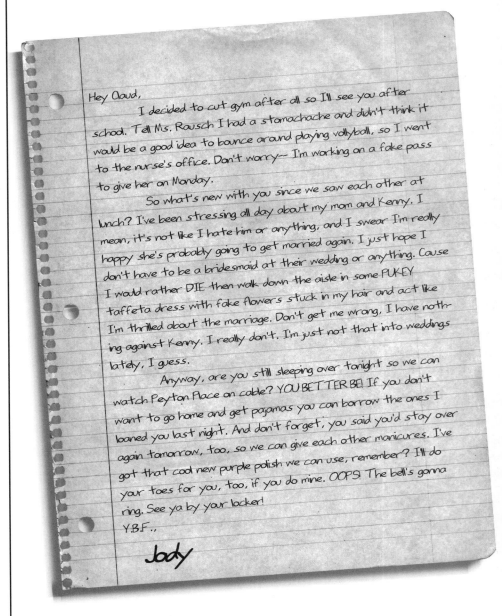

Hey Claud,

I decided to cut gym after all so I'll see you after school. Tell Ms. Rausch I had a stomachache and didn't think it would be a good idea to bounce around playing volleyball, so I went to the nurse's office. Don't worry— I'm working on a fake pass to give her on Monday.

So what's new with you since we saw each other at lunch? I've been stressing all day about my mom and Kenny. I mean, it's not like I hate him or anything, and I swear I'm really happy she's probably going to get married again. I just hope I don't have to be a bridesmaid at their wedding or anything. Cause I would rather DIE then walk down the aisle in some PUKEY taffeta dress with fake flowers stuck in my hair and act like I'm thrilled about the marriage. Don't get me wrong, I have nothing against Kenny. I really don't. I'm just not that into weddings lately, I guess.

Anyway, are you still sleeping over tonight so we can watch Peyton Place on cable? YOU BETTER BE! If you don't want to go home and get pajamas you can borrow the ones I loaned you last night. And don't forget, you said you'd stay over again tomorrow, too, so we can give each other manicures. I've got that cool new purple polish we can use, remember? I'll do your toes for you, too, if you do mine. OOPS! The bell's gonna ring. See ya by your locker!

Y.B.F.,

Jody

A Family Album   63

KIRSTEN

It was last year. Last December... Right after the wedding... What can I tell you, the holidays were—They were bad. What did you expect? ...I went to see someone.

CHARLIE

Dr. Leto?

KIRSTEN

I saw him for awhile. And he gave me those pills, and I took them for—for a couple of months. And then I stopped. I'm fine, Charlie. I'm...

CHARLIE

That's when all this stuff happened, isn't it? With your dissertation?

KIRSTEN

They kept calling me. "Where's your dissertation? You're late." ...I couldn't get out of bed. It was like—it was like—you know the fog in the morning? The way it comes in and just... I don't even remember typing those paragraphs. But I must have.

CHARLIE

Did I do this to you?

Dr. Jerome Kass
Doctoral Advisor, Department of Psychology
San Francisco State University ● San Francisco ● California ● 94132

Ms. Kirsten Bennett
3324 Broadway
San Francisco, Ca

October 1, 1996

Dear Ms. Bennett:

In reference to our conversation this morning, this letter confirms that you have admitted to committing plagiarism in your dissertation.

This case will be turned over to an advisory committee for review, and a meeting will be scheduled for next week. Unfortunately, there is a strong possibility that your Ph.D. will be revoked.

I would like to offer my genuine regret, Ms. Bennett, about this most unfortunate situation. My office will notify you of the committee's decision.

Sincerely

Jerome Kass

Jerome Kass
Professor of Psychology

CLAUDIA

Charlie's room, where he called off the wedding. *That* was fun. This was Bailey's. Something bad's always happening to him. Julia's old room at the end. Miscarriage. Oh. And this is the bathroom. Bailey's girlfriend Jill stole some drugs in there...

DR. BLALOCK

And what happened to *her?*

CLAUDIA

Give you one guess... —and this is where I found Kirsten crying one time. She came down here because she thought nobody could hear, but it went up through the heating ducts and it sounded like the whole house was sobbing. Only now she's gone and it's all my fault and Charlie hates me and I have to do something...

DR. BLALOCK

A vortex of negative forces. I'm getting something—what's in this box?

CLAUDIA

Some stuff of my parents'. They died three years ago... So...you think we need an exorcism?

SARAH

I know what's going on.

BAILEY

Going on? Nothing's going on...

SARAH

Please don't lie to me, okay? Cause that's only gonna make it worse...

BAILEY

Lie to you? Why would I lie to you?

SARAH

I should have seen it coming. You're in college now and I'm still stuck in high school and—we're at different stages in our lives, and we have totally different needs now—

BAILEY

Listen, Sarah, I can explain—

SARAH

—so I can't really blame you for being mad at me.

BAILEY

Mad? At you?

SARAH

I mean, I'm practically forcing you to go to this stupid dance. It's so totally high school, and of course you don't want to go, so, you know what? You don't have to. It's okay... I mean, that's it, right?

BAILEY

No. I mean, yes.

GRANT HIGH SCHOOL
is proud to present
The Fifth Annual

CHARITY COSTUME BALL

Halloween Night in the Gymnasium
8 p.m until the Witching Hour

Featuring:
Faculty Lookalike Jack O'Lantern Patch
Cash Prizes for the Best Costumes
Souvenir Pictures
Music by D.J. Doozie's Sound Machine
Monster Mash Dance Contest
Refreshments

Tickets: $5.00 Presale/$7.5
All proceeds to benefit the Children's
Committee Chairwoman: Sarah Reeves

Bailey—
Are you planning on coming to this with me or not? We really have to talk. Please call me.
—Sarah

Dear Charlie,
 I just received the boxes you sent. Thank you so much for taking the time to pack up all my things and ship them to me. I haven't opened them. I'm not ready to do that yet. Maybe I'll never be ready or maybe I won't have to open them here. Maybe I'll be able to ship them right back to San Francisco some time soon, where they belong. Where I belong.
 There are so many things I want to say to you about what happened, but I can't put any of it down on paper. I started seeing Dr. Leto again, to help me sort out my thoughts. He said it's going to take a lot of time and for me to be patient with myself. He put me on new medication, more antidepressants. I guess they're working; at least I've been able to get out of bed in the morning.
 Charlie, I don't know what else to say except that I miss you and I love you. And I'm sorry.

 Kirsten

KIRSTEN
I'm...sorry. I—
CHARLIE
No. Don't be. It's okay. Really... Actually, it's probably for the best. This way, all you have to do is concentrate on getting better. You won't have the five of us stomping up and down those stairs all day, and Owen screaming and the dog barking and me and Bay yelling at each other, and— Hey, don't cry. Please don't cry.
KIRSTEN
You're crying.
CHARLIE
However long it takes. I'm not going anywhere... I love you. You know that, don't you?... Don't you?... Could you...could you say it? Just so I know you really know.
KIRSTEN
You love me.
CHARLIE
You gotta remember to bundle up this winter. You know Chicago...

Stanford University
English Department

Ms. Julia Salinger
3324 Broadway
San Francisco, CA

November 3, 1996

Dear Julia:

I took a look at your work, and here are my thoughts. It won't help if I sugarcoat this, so I'm not going to. And it's not to say that you won't improve over time.

But for now, I think you should hold off submitting the piece with your application. There's an awkwardness to the language and an unfocused quality in the storytelling that makes the piece feel, for lack of a better phrase, very young. Even your choice of second-person narration seems a juvenile contribution, rather than creating the sophisticated tone you were obviously aiming for.

I've jotted in the margins of the story— I'm afraid I went a little overboard and rewrote some of the passages on the backs of the pages, just to give you an idea of the kind of effect you should be trying to achieve. If you wish to discuss this with me, you can leave a message on my home machine—555-2783—and we'll get together and talk.

Sincerely,

Gary Prescott

GARY
I've seen you before. Were you— you were at my reading at Green Apple last Thursday.

JULIA
I also saw you at City Lights. Your stuff—it just—it gets in, you know? I read it, or I hear you reading it, and then I have to just sit and let it kick around in my head. If I could ever write anything even *close* to "Dog With a Bone"...

GARY
A writer, huh?

JULIA
Kind of. Since I was, I don't know, in second grade. I'm—I'm meeting at Stanford this week, with somebody in Admissions. I'm hoping I can beg my way into the creative writing program.

GARY
No kidding? I teach in that department.

JULIA

Mom, Charlie. Mom took these pictures.

CHARLIE

Really? where'd you find them?

JULIA

With her stuff from Stanford. This is what she majored in—visual arts. *Not* music.

CHARLIE

Huh. That's—I didn't know that.

JULIA

Me, either...I was thinking about her all day yesterday. After I messed up the interview. I kept thinking, there was Mom, and *she* went to Stanford and she knew exactly what she wanted to be when she was my age—and—and I kinda didn't, anymore. I kept—I kept apologizing to her, in my head. Like maybe I let her down. And then I found these...in a box of her stuff. It's like she's telling me that it's okay. That I don't have to be a hundred percent sure today, this minute, of who I'm gonna be. Cause she was searching too.

Mr. Gary Prescott
English Department
Stanford University
Stanford, California 94305

November 8, 1996

Dear Gary:

Thank you for reading my story, and for your criticism. You definitely gave me a lot to think about.

I have this habit—I've always done this—whenever I get a new book, I turn to the last page first. Because I need to know how things are going to turn out. I've decided I'm not going to do that anymore. And maybe I wouldn't have figured that out if I hadn't met you. I don't know if that's going to make sense to you or not, but I think that's really what I'm thanking you for.

As for what you said about my work—maybe you're right. But maybe you aren't. And maybe I will become a writer and maybe I won't. I don't know.

I haven't read the last page yet.

Sincerely,

Julia Salinger

Julia Salinger

Bailey—
Here's the phone bill. I circled my long distance calls. Some of they are Ray's. If you figure out what you owe I'll track Ray down for his share and pay it off Monday.

I found that sweater you were looking for—it got mixed in with my laundry. I folded it & put it on your bed.

Also, we're out of roach spray again, and I saw a monster one crawling in the bathtub this morning. I was thinking we should get some of those trap things instead of spray. Maybe we should go grocery shopping together this time, so we can split the bill. That way, we won't end up with all those doubles of stuff we both use.

Anyway, I'll be home after my late lab, by nine at the latest. So if you don't have important plans with Sarah, wait for me and we'll hit the Stop 'N Shop together. I hate to disrupt your social life— maybe we can stop for a beer on the way home or something.
Later—
Callie

BAILEY
My underwear.
Where's my under-
wear?
CALLIE
I chucked 'em into
the fireplace, I
think. Why so mod-
est? C'mere.
BAILEY
No. I don't think—
Callie. I can't
believe—how could—
what *was* that? Huh?
What just happened
here?
CALLIE
Gee. I dunno...
sex?
BAILEY
This wasn't—what
does this mean?
CALLIE
It means we had
sex. And I don't
know about you, but
I had a good
time...
BAILEY
We shouldn't have
done that. We just—
we shouldn't have
done that.

Claudia Salinger's
Famous Ants on a Log

Ingredients

One bunch celery
One container soft cream cheese
One small box of raisins

Wash celery well and peel off stringy things. Chop off top of stem that has leaves and bottom of stem where its all flat and white. Carefully spread inside of stalk with cream cheese. Stick raisins along the cream cheese. Eat.

HOMELESS EJECTED FROM EATERY

BY J. TORRES
STAFF REPORTER

Eleven homeless people were asked to leave Salinger's Restaurant last night after they showed up for dinner as guests of Jim Seely, a San Francisco performance artist.

Seely, the winner of the restaurant's recent slogan contest, was there to redeem part of his prize: fifty-two coupons for free dinners at Salinger's. Charles Salinger, the restaurant manager, was reportedly disturbed when Seely arrived at the restaurant with several homeless people in tow.

"He asked us to leave when patrons at nearby tables started making faces at my friends," Seely commented. "... bothering any... to eat ... st like ... body

...ding to ...ayne, a ...ear-old ...ent, Mr. ...inger ...d him boldly out the door.

Seely, Payne, and several others involved are considering bringing charges against Mr. Salinger, who has been running the family-owned restaurant for the past year.

Grace Wilcox, who runs San Francisco's Harvest Program, said, "Mr. Salinger's actions are reprehensible. I contacted him several times recently to ask if he would consider donating leftover food to the homeless, and each time, he claimed to be too busy or too distracted to talk to me. Now it's apparent why he couldn't be bothered. He apparently feels disdain for the poor, starving people of this city."

Ms. Wilcox is planning to organize a boycott of Salinger's restaurant.

When reached at the family's Broadway residence, thirteen-year-old Claudia Salinger disavowed her brother's actions. "If my father was alive, I doubt he would have handled it this way."

Charles Salinger could not be reached for comment.

GRACE
You want to help? I'm an advocate for the poor, Charlie. I don't go out on a limb for people like you.

CHARLIE
People like—What's that supposed to mean?

GRACE
Salinger's—it's been here for a couple of decades. Who started it? Dad?

CHARLIE
Yeah. It was my father's. Why?

GRACE
So how'd that work? You got to be twenty-two, and Daddy called you into the study and said, "Son, I think it's time for you to take over the business." And boom—you're set for life.

CHARLIE
I'm sorry, but—who do you think you are?

GRACE
This may be news, Charlie, but the world is full of people who haven't had their lives handed to them on a silver platter. Most have had to struggle for what they have. And lots of times, in order to make it, they need people taking care of them.

CHARLIE
And you can tell, from looking at me, that I don't know anything about taking care of people?

GRACE
Yeah. I can... What? You gonna tell me I'm wrong?

CHARLIE
God, no. You're never wrong.

The Sampler

Walt Whitman Junior High　　　　**November 1996 Issue**

"I, Claudia... Advice to the Lovelorn"

I'm a ninth grader and I have a major problem. I've noticed lately that all my friends are into girls, like talking about them and asking them out and everything. And I'm not into it at all. I'm kind of into—well, I think I might be gay. And I'm terrified someone's going to find out about it and think I'm some sort of freak. Please help me. This is ruining my life.
Signed,
Confused at Fourteen

Dear Claudia:
I'm in seventh grade, and I have a crush on this ninth grader. But he doesn't know I exist. I think about him all the time. Sometimes, I can't even get to sleep at night because he's on my mind. What should I do?
Signed,
Invisible

Dear Invisible:
Go for it. Life's too short. <u>Force</u> him to notice you. Spill your guts and at least then you'll know where you stand.

Dear Claudia:

Dear Confused:
You're not the problem. The problem is that you don't have anybody to talk to because you're too hung up on what other people will think. Being gay is nothing to be ashamed of. People we all know and respect—family, friends, even one of Whitman's most popular teachers—are homosexual. You need to single out someone you can trust—a parent, sibling, friend, or teacher—and confide in them. You'll feel much better and take the first steps toward embracing the real you.

CLAUDIA
So what's the big deal? They asked and I told. It's junior high. Not the military.

ROSS
That's not—it's a big deal for Paul, okay? He didn't want to bring his personal life into his job and he didn't give you permission to do it for him!

CLAUDIA
How was I s'posed to know. You never said it was a *secret.*

ROSS
Only because it never occurred to me you'd print it in the damn newspaper!

CLAUDIA
But I didn't even use his name! And you read that kid's letter, Ross. He signed it "Confused at Fourteen" for a reason...

ROSS
I know. I know. And what he's going through is hard, but that still doesn't mean—

CLAUDIA
I was just trying to tell him he's not alone. And—I thought Mr. Archer would be like this really positive example... But obviously, I was wrong. What I should have said is he'd be better off *lying* for the rest of his life...

WILL
It seems like all you want to do anymore is drink.

BAILEY
What? Welcome to college, Will. It's—kinda part of it.

WILL
I know. I know that, but—my point is—it's just—you're drinking a lot. Like...a *lot*.

BAILEY
Yeah? Especially since you've been here but—I thought we were—you got some kind of problem with that?

WILL
More to the point, Bay...do you?

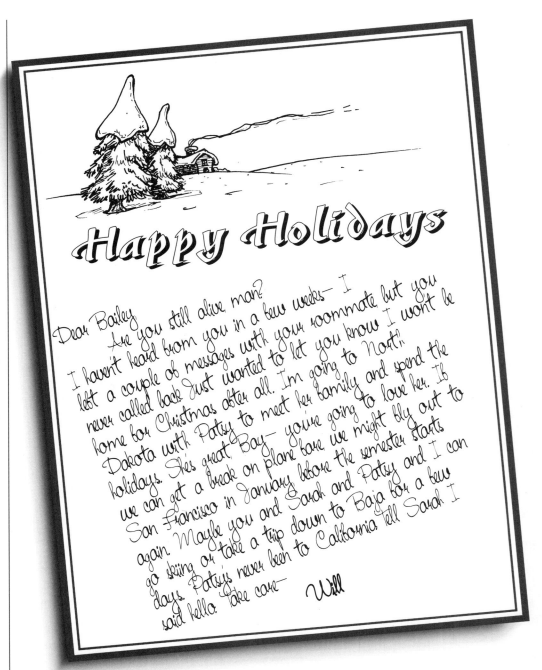

Happy Holidays

Dear Bailey,
Are you still alive, man? I haven't heard from you in a few weeks— I left a couple of messages with your roommate but you never called back. Just wanted to let you know I won't be home for Christmas after all. I'm going to North Dakota with Patsy to meet her family and spend the holidays. She's great, Bay— you're going to love her. If we can get a break on plane fare, we might fly out to San Francisco in January before the semester starts again. Maybe you and Sarah and Patsy and I can go skiing or take a trip down to Baja for a few days. Patsy's never been to California. Tell Sarah I said hello. Take care—
Will

Dear Claudia,
This necklace belonged to my mother, your great-grandmother. She was a great music-lover and would be happy to know it was being worn by her great-granddaughter the violinist.
Merry Christmas.
Love,
Grandpa

CHARLIE
What kind of appoint-
ment could you have on
Christmas morning?

JAKE
A chemo appointment...
It's cancer, Charlie.

CHARLIE
Jake, I'm...sorry,
God...what can we do, I
mean, there has to be
something—

JAKE
No, look, I'm okay.
I've got enough money.
I've got a good doctor.
It's gonna be okay.

CHARLIE
But—you'll come back,
right? I mean—let us
help. We're family...

JAKE
If I spend Christmas
here, those kids will
only get more attached.
And then, when I go—So
I tell you what. You
kids have Christmas the
way you've always had
it. No new traditions
for me.

CHARLIE
Claudia was so excited
to have you here.

JAKE
I know. She's gonna be
mad. But she can handle
that better than she
can handle losing me.
Don't you think?

CLAUDIA

Look. Stuart. You're a nice guy, but—there isn't going to be any future for us. I don't like you like that.

STUART

But—that present—

CLAUDIA

—was supposed to be impersonal. How was I supposed to know it would mean something? What kind of person collects those things?

STUART

My kind.

CLAUDIA

I'm sorry. That came out wrong—

STUART

Wow. Here I thought you were this nice person...

CLAUDIA

I *am* nice—

STUART

No, you're not. Nice people don't lead people on, then squash their hearts like a bug.

BAILEY
If you've got a prob-
lem—just say it.
SARAH
Nothing. It's just...
"Happy Birthday. I
love you, Bailey."
That's it? That's all
you wanted to say?

BAILEY
It's a birthday card.
I wrote happy birth-
day.

SARAH
Right. And you wrote
the word "love" too.
That's romantic!
That's really heart-
felt! How long did
that take you?

BAILEY
What is your
problem?

SARAH
I don't know. Maybe
it's that I write
these long funny
things to you on your
birthday—these really
romantic things. So
it feels like, I
don't know... Is
there something
you're trying to say
to me?

BAILEY
I wrote "I love
you!" What do you
think I'm trying to
say to you?

SARAH
Forget it.

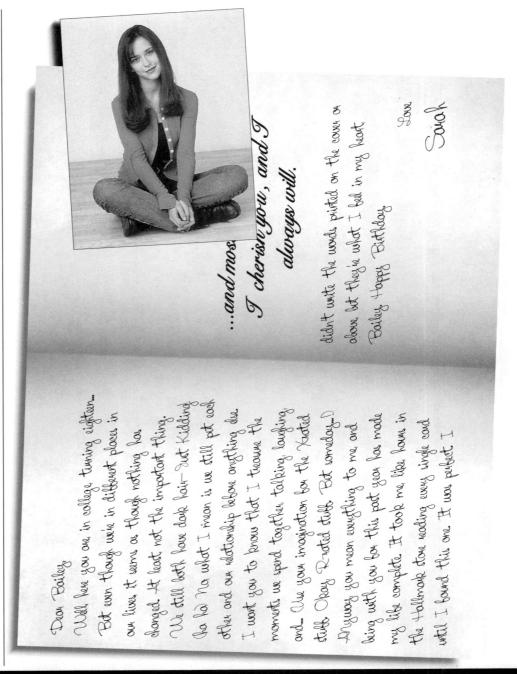

Dear Bailey,

Well here you are in college turning eighteen...

But even though we're in different places in our lives, it seems as though nothing has changed. At least not the important thing.

We still both have dark hair—but kidding

Ha ha ha, what I mean is we still put each other and our relationship above anything else. I want you to know that I treasure the moments we spend together, talking, laughing and... Use your imagination for the X-rated stuff. Okay X-rated stuff. But someday...:)

Anyway you mean everything to me and being with you for this past year has made my life complete. It took me like hours in the Hallmark store reading every single card until I found this one. It was perfect. I

didn't write the words printed on the cover or above but they're what I feel in my heart

Bailey, Happy Birthday.

Love,
Sarah

...and mos
I cherish you, and I
always will.

In 200 words or less, describe where you plan to be ten years in the future:

It isn't easy for me to answer this question, because I don't necessarily believe in "planning" the future. At one time I did; I thought I would always know exactly what tomorrow would hold for me. I figured I would always be shy Julia Salinger, the A-student with the nice, "normal" family: Mom, Dad, and five of us kids.

Then, when I was fifteen, things changed. Mom and Dad were gone overnight. The rest of us struggled to stay together. My grades started slipping. I stopped trying to get lost in the background; I learned to reach out to people. And I realized that no matter how much you try to plan—how much you *want* to plan for the future, it's impossible.

So—where do I *hope* to be in ten years from now? I hope to have an undergraduate degree under my belt; maybe even a master's. I hope to be making a living as a writer—or at least, making a living. And I hope that the people in my life today—the people I love more than anyt_____ll continue to surround me. Because, in the grand scheme of things, that's what counts.

SAM
This is something you want.

JULIA
Really? When did I decide that? When did I weigh my options and say, yes, *college*. Never. It's just been *assumed*. By everyone—my family, my teachers. *Me*.

SAM
Okay. Okay, so maybe you need to decide that. Think it through.

JULIA
I'm *trying*. I keep telling myself it's a great opportunity, but—for what? For proving yet again that I'm a good student? I know that. It's like, the only thing I know about myself. And—so what? It's not like that means anything. How well you do in school is not who you are.

SAM
So—you don't want to go... Hey. It's okay to say you've had it with school.

JULIA
I think—I think I've had it with school. I think I don't want to go... Huh.

SAM
What?

JULIA
I feel...a little less like I'm gonna throw up.

JULIA

I don't know if Libby would say, "keep going." I kind of think she'd say, stop. Stop and—make sure that the stuff you're doing right now—right now—is really what makes you happy. You know? I'm—I'm trying to—to find something to take from this. Cause otherwise, all it is, is that my friend is dead. And that's... The thing is, you can't just live for some—some goal in the future, or have that be everything, have it be *it*. Cause that's what she did. It's like she got on—not really, but like, this road. And there were all these signs, "this way, this way." But what if you get there, what if you get exactly what you wanted—like Libby did—except all the things that are wrong are still wrong? Then what? God, Libby. I'm sorry you were so unhappy. I'll miss you.

February 1997 — Grant H

Promising Senior Commits Suicide

BY SEAN DAVIDSON

Not everyone at Grant High knew Libby Dwyer. She wasn't the kind of person you'd expect to find leading cheers at a pep rally or being voted Most Outgoing in the class superlative poll. Libby was quiet, and nice, and smart. So smart it seemed her whole future was all sewn up. Maybe that was the problem.

On January 6, Libby returned to school after Christmas break and informed her friends that she had been accepted to Harvard, early-decision. Those with whom she shared the news have commented that she didn't seem ecstatic, or even pleased.

"I thought she seemed kind of distracted," says Justin Thompson, who used to date Libby, looking back on that fateful day. "It was like she didn't even want to talk about it."

On the night of January 6, Libby swallowed a handful of sleeping pills, then went into the garage of the house where she lived with her mother. She closed the door, climbed into the car, and started the engine.

When her mother found her early next morning, she had already died. She didn't leave a note.

Julia Salinger, who was one of Libby's closest friends when they were younger but admits the two had drifted apart recently, commented, "I think it was the fact that she got accepted to Harvard that made her do it. She couldn't handle the pressure. It was too much to live up to...so she chose not to live at all."

Salinger, who gave a moving eulogy at Libby's funeral last month, has organized a scholarship fund in memory of her late friend. A meeting for anyone interested in being on the committee will be held after school in the auditorium on Monday February 10.

Bailey Salinger

Page 1

Intro to Poetry

An In-Depth Analysis of T.S. Eliot's
"The Love song of J. Alfred Prufrock"

Although I felt like it ran on forever, this poem can be totally summed up in one sentence: Prufrock thinks it's a freaky world, where sometimes you need a little fantasy to help figure out how to deal with reality.

The way I see it, Prufrock is just this middle-aged guy who's not all there. you can trell he's middle-ages because of the line, "With a bald spot in the middle od my hair," and because toward the end he repeats, "I grow old... I grow old." It's ike he's bummed out about the owkr world,and he does a lot of thinking about yewllow smopke and yellow fog, whcih shows he's not living in the real world, where smoke and fog are gray. There are also many referenceces to sleep, which is cleverly contrasted by several mentions of caffinated beverages such as coffee (mentioned once) and tea (four times).

When the poet T.S. Eliot writed, "Like a patient etherized upon a table," he meant seems to be daying that ther eis a patient,a nd there is a table, and he is on it, the patient, and he is also on a substance, most likely either.

tydf

CALLIE
So how's the paper coming? Seems like you got a lot done.

BAILEY
Tons. I did tons. I got quotes, I got footnotes, I got arguments arguing with arguments...

CALLIE
Ten pages yet?

BAILEY
Well, incentive plan called for a beer a page, so that means—counting your two there—

CALLIE
Eleven pages? Bailey, that's great!

BAILEY
Well, yeah—give or take... Cause you know, every plan has its fine print. Like this beer right here... This's for a bitchin' symbol thing I found in one of those stanzas. And this one's just a bonus beer for setting a personal record—180 minutes of consecutive studying. And this one, I'm not exactly—oops—

CALLIE
What are you? Totally drunk?

BAILEY
I'm inspired by your greatness, Cal. If you can write like this with five beers, think what I can do with fifteen!

SARAH
Are you crying? What's—what happened?

JULIA
Everything. It's just so—screwed up.

SARAH
Can you, like, be more specific?

JULIA
Bailey. He ruined Owen's party. He was so awful...

SARAH
Oh my God. Was he drunk?

JULIA
For, like, five minutes yesterday, he was himself. Then—he drinks and just...turns into this—Oh, God, Sarah. This is really bad, isn't it?

SARAH
Is he still here?

JULIA
Passed out.

IT'S A PARTY!

For: Owen Salinger

Occasion: Third Birthday

When: Saturday, 2 p.m.–4 p.m.

Where: 3324 Broadway, San Francisco

RSVP: Charlie, 555-7824

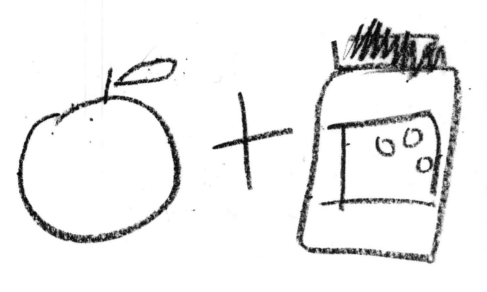

Owen's Favorite Recipe
Apples with Peanut Butter

Ingredients

1 medium-sized apple
1 glob creamy peanut butter

Have a brother or sister wash, peel, and core the apple, then slice it into small pieces. Place peanut butter on plate, arrange apple chunks around it. Dip apple into peanut butter. Eat!

JOE

Why do you insist on only looking for the bad stuff, Bailey? You really think I showed up at your house and told you about your Dad's drinking because I wanted to make things worse for you? I told you because I thought it would give you a little hope! Yeah—you got what made your Dad start drinking. But if you'd just *look* for it—you've got what made him stop too!

BAILEY

You know what—?!

CLAUDIA

Why not? Why isn't it possible? Maybe you got all the stuff that made us love him...and made Mom love him... Maybe you got *all* of him...

BAILEY

I don't—What does this have to do with God, anyway?

JOE

Are you kidding me? Are you *kidding* me? Your father didn't disappear. He's inside of you. And that doesn't just *happen*. If the world were random and mean—like you think it is... I think it's proof that there's someone or something looking out for us.

BAILEY

I don't know.

JOE

It's not a curse, Bailey. It's a gift—if you look at it that way... And every time you fight the urge to drink—every time you beat the urge to drink—you feel him. And you know he didn't really leave you when he died. He's still here... You're not alone, Bailey.

A.A. Serenity Prayer
God grant me the serenity to accept the things I cannot change, the courage to change the things I can, and the wisdom to know the difference.

AMAZING GRACE:
CANDIDATE WILCOX KICKS OFF CAMPAIGN

BY COLLEEN GRAY
STAFF REPORTER

A visit to her campaign headquarters-slash-home is enough to convince anyone that homeless advocate Grace Wilcox isn't your typical politician.

After losing her Tenderloin apartment to a recent fire, the single city council candidate accepted boyfriend Charlie Salinger's offer to take up residence in a sprawling three-story Victorian in an upscale neighborhood—and suddenly found herself living family life to its fullest. Despite her full-time job with the Harvest Program and the pressures of running for office, Wilcox still manages to find quiet time with her domestic partner and his four younger siblings.

Salinger, manager of Salinger's Restaurant on Union Street and a consultant on the Wilcox Campaign, became guardian of his brothers and sisters after their parents were killed in a drunk-driving accident three years ago. This dashing young father figure admits that the younger Salingers have long needed a female role model—and that Wilcox has stepped smoothly into the position. According to Salinger, his youngest brother, Owen, 3, took an immediate liking to the candidate, and his three teenage siblings followed suit.

One afternoon in the busy kitchen, which doubles as the nerve center for the campaign, Wilcox expertly juggled phone calls from the mayor's office with Owen's story time, keeping her cool even when the toddler toppled his juice box, spilling sticky purple liquid over an important fax. Indeed, her slogan "Grace Under Pressure" seems an apt description.

As her grassroots campaign picks up momentum, this capable nineties woman shows no sign of slowing down—or neglecting the motherless children who have come to depend on her. And at least two local organizations—Friends of Alternative Families and Single Mothers' Action League (S.M.A.L.)—have taken notice.

"It's refreshing to see a female politician who isn't afraid to show her nurturing, maternal side," said Joanna Thompson, a spokeswoman for the S.M.A.L., which has endorsed Wilcox's candidacy. "Grace Wilcox demonstrates that it really is possible to have it all."

CLAUDIA
Owen's having a good time, so... Why don't we stay a little longer? We never get quality time together, so... We could check out the... *Dinosaurs—*

GRACE
I've got to find a phone. If there's been some kind of mix up, I don't want to waste any more time.

CLAUDIA
That's what this is to you? A waste of time?

GRACE
That's not—you know what I mean. C'mon. I want to call. If there's no reporter, we should do go.

CLAUDIA
There's no reporter... I made it up to prove a point.

GRACE
What? What are you talking about?

CLAUDIA
I just knew the only way you'd ever spend any time with us is if you thought you'd get something out of it... And apparently I was right.

CLAUDIA

Do you know what a big deal tonight was? Do you know how scary it is to stand up in front of a thousand people who've heard the Bartok a zillion times, only played by Isaac Stern or Itzack Perlman. It's, like, hard to breathe and your fingers feel all thick—and you feel—you feel—

BAILEY

What?

CLAUDIA

Alone. I felt alone. I can't count on you anymore. And I can't *go* to you to make me feel better, because you're... All of a sudden, I'm like the one taking care of *you*, cleaning up after you, looking out for you, and *it's not fair*.

BAILEY

Why not? Why isn't that fair? Because I'm older than you? Because you need taking care of and I don't? Would you STOP?! Look, I'm a mess. I've got a real problem here and I'm try-ing—I'm fighting this thing and I wish you didn't have to watch me do it—but you do. That's just how it is... You're not a baby anymore. And you're not gonna be a kid for too much longer. Maybe you could come through for *me*.

===Los Angeles Chamber Orchestra===

Ms. Claudia Salinger
3324 Broadway
San Francisco, California

March 8, 1997

Dear Ms. Salinger:

I am pleased to inform y_____ ___ __ave been selected as one of three violinists to perform with the Los Angeles Chamber Orchestra in the Fourth Annual Young Soloists Series. We invite you and a chaperon to fly to Los Angeles the week of April 7, where you will engage in a series of rehearsals before the performance on Saturday, April 12 at the Music Center. We will cover expenses for you and your guest, including plane fare, hotel costs, and meals.

We request that you inform us by March 15 if you plan to accept this invitation.

Sincerely,

Marjorie Newman

Marjorie Newman
Chairman
Young Soloists Series
PO Box 1893
Los Angeles, California 90052

*Bailey,
This is the letter with all the information about the trip to LA— I'm so excited that you're coming with me! I called Joe and he'll meet us after the performance and take us out to dinner. But maybe we can still get room service for breakfast!*
Claudia

CHARLIE

There's no way you woulda done something like this if Mom and Dad—

JULIA

—No, maybe not. But if they *had* been here these past few years—I'd be like, someone else entirely. I'm who I am *because* they died, Charlie—I mean, that's made me me.

CHARLIE

So, what, you run off and get *married*? Have you even *thought* about what that means?

JULIA

Of course.

CHARLIE

For how long? A minute? An hour? Did you even know yesterday you were getting married today?

JULIA

I thought about it when he asked me. And when I said yes, it felt like the rightest thing I've ever done in my life. It felt like with that word, everything just snapped into place. It's like—Griffin loves me and we're going to be together forever, which means I can go anywhere, do anything, and I'll have that, I'll have him. And I love *him*—so he can stop worrying he's going to lose me, and just relax, and become this—this man he's kinda waiting to be.

CERTIF...   N

City of San Francisco

This is to certify that the persons identified below were married on the date and at the place specified as shown by the duly registered license and certificate of marriage on file in this office.

GROOM
Name: Griffin Holbrook
Residing at: San Francisco, California
Date of Birth: July 5, 1978
Place of Birth: Fort Bragg, NC

BRIDE
Name: Julia Gordon Salinger
New Surname (if applicable): Julia Salinger Holbrook
Residing at: San Francisco, CA
Date of Birth: May 10, 1979
Place of Birth: San Francisco, CA

Date of Marriage: June 14., 1997

Place of Marriage: San Francisco, CA

City Clerk: *Elaine I. Johnson* — June 13, 1997

GRACE

God, Charlie, maybe it's not just add water and instant parent. Maybe it takes time.

CHARLIE

Okay, but—but what if we do that? We give it time, and you try and then you go, "nope, not for me"? And Owen's four? Or five?

GRACE

Do you hear what you're asking me? Why do I have to predict the future all of a sudden?

CHARLIE

I have to. Cause he's gonna miss you, but you know what? Now he's little. A couple of months, he won't remember. So now is—it's safe.

GRACE

Charlie—

CHARLIE

If this was about you and me, if this was just about right now, if I didn't have to think about... I mean, I love you, Grace.

GRACE

But that's it? You're just gonna give this up? And—and—and put them ahead of everything you said you want? Put them ahead of you?

CHARLIE

That's what parents do.

Wilcox defeats Katz for council seat

BY AIDAN ARMSTRONG-ROBERTSON
STAFF REPORTER

In a stunning upset, political newcomer Grace Wilcox beat long-time San Francisco politician Alfred Katz for a seat on the city council.

Wilcox, a homeless advocate whose grassroots campaign was run from the home of her domestic partner and consultant Charlie Salinger, was initially dismissed by Katz as a "one-issue candidate." But while her platform did indeed focus on social issues involving the city's poor, she proved to be a formidable opponent for Katz, knowledgeable on a broad spectrum of pertinent concerns and capturing not just the minority vote, but a large segment of female voters as well, thanks to her position as a maternal role model in a household made of Salinger's younger siblings, four motherless orphans.

Throughout the campaign, Wilcox has displayed a tremendous amount of energy. When asked last night how she planned to celebrate her victory, the suddenly weary-looking councilwoman-elect answered, with her trademark straightforward honesty, "Sleep."